FANFARE FOR ELIZABETH

EDITH SITWELL

Fanfare for Elizabeth

PETER OWEN · LONDON

ISBN 0 7206 0732 9

PETER OWEN PUBLISHERS
73 Kenway Road London SW5 0RE

First published 1946
This edition published 1989
© 1945, 1946 Francis Sitwell

Printed in Great Britain by Billings of Worcester

To Pavel Tchelitchew

ILLUSTRATIONS

(between pages 106 and 107)

Queen Elizabeth

Anne Boleyn

Catherine Howard

King Henry VIII and his children

ACKNOWLEDGEMENTS

My thanks are due to Mrs Violet Gordon Woodhouse for her great kindness in playing to me, with her inimitable art, some of the music mentioned in this book — including King Henry's "O Western Wind" — and to Lord Grey de Ruthyn for his untiring help and advice, and for having placed his great learning in matters connected to this age at my disposal. I have also to express my indebtedness to Messrs Longmans, Green & Co., Ltd, for allowing me to reprint extracts from Professor A. F. Pollard's *Henry VIII*. References to other works from which incidental quotations have been taken will be found in the Notes at the end of each chapter.

Chapter One

THIS is England, this is the Happy Isle ; it is the year 1533 and we are on our way to the country palace of the King — a giant with a beard of gold and a will of iron. . . . " If a lion knew his strength," said Sir Thomas More to Cromwell, of his master, " it were hard to rule him." Henry the Eighth had that leonine strength, but he had also a strange wisdom that was like a third eye, seeing into the hearts of his people. He was born to rule, and with all his lion's strength and ferocity he was in certain ways a great King — averting from England many of the storms that arose in Europe from the changes in religious opinion. But his blindness in one direction was as great as his seeing powers in another, and he did not avert poverty from his people. On the contrary, he brought down destitution upon thousands by the overthrow of the monasteries.

He was a man of great personal beauty : " His Majesty ", wrote the Venetian, Sebastiano Giustinian, " is as handsome as nature could form, above any Christian prince — handsomer far than the King of France. He is exceedingly fair, and as well proportioned as possible. When he learned that the King of France wore a beard, he allowed his to grow ; which being somewhat red, has the appearance of being of gold. . . . Affable and benign, he offends no one. He has often said to the Ambassador that he wished that everyone was content with his own condition, adding that ' we are content with our islands '."

He drew the bow, declared the Ambassador, with greater force than any man in Europe, and jousted marvellously. As late as 1529, a new ambassador, Falier, said that " In the eighth Henry God has combined such corporeal and intellectual beauty as not merely to surprise but astound all men. His face is angelic rather than handsome."

Even in his later years Henry had still an appearance of great magnificence and power, like a sun running to seed. But he had grown heavier, the earth shook when he walked. And the prince with the face of an angel had fallen under the spell of his own princely will.

His temper had changed ; but in earlier days he seemed a part of the English soil, of the English air, which was so mild that "laurel and rosemary flourish all winter, especially in the southern parts, and in summer time England yields apricots plentifully, musk melons in good quantity, and figs in some places, all of which ripen well, and by the same reason, all beasts bring forth their young in the open fields, even in the time of winter. And England hath such abundance of apples, pears, cherries and plums, such variety of them and so good in all respects, that no country yields more or better, for which the Italians would gladly exchange their citrons and oranges. But upon the sea coasts the winds many times blast the fruits in the very flower. . . ." [1]

At the end of Elizabeth's reign, "Besides that we have most delicate apples, plummes, peares, walnuts, filberds, etc.," wrote Harrison,[2] "and those of sundrie sorts, planted within fortie yeeres passed, in comparison with which most of the old trees are nothing worth, have we no less store of strange fruit, as abricots, almonds, peaches, figges, corne-trees" (a kind of cherry) "in noble men's orchards. I have seene capers, oranges and lemmons, and heard of wild olives growing here ; besides the strange trees, brought from far, whose names I know not. . . . We have in like sort such workmen as are not onlie excellent in graffing the naturall fruits, but also in their artificial mixtures, whereby one tree bringeth forth sundrie fruits, and one and the same fruit of divers colours and tastes, dalleing as it were with nature and his course, as if his whole trade were perfectlie known unto them : of hard fruits they will make tender, of soure sweet, of sweet yet more delicate, bereaving, also some of their kernels, others of their cores, and finally induing them with the savour of muske, ambre, or sweet spices at their pleasures. Divers also have written at large of these severall practises, and some of them had to convert the kernels of peaches into almonds, of small fruit to make farre greater, and to remove or add superfluous moisture to the trees."

Gardens and orchards containing fruits such as these, grew in the heart of London.

It was thought, earlier in the giant's reign, that gold lay under the soil. . . . But that hope proved to be unfounded. There were, however, other riches. Polydore Vergil had called the wool yielded by those sheep " that bring forth their young in the open fields ", " England's Golden Fleece ".[3] All was fatness and plenty, until the nation of the beggars began with the destitution caused by the suppression of the monasteries.

What is that rumbling noise we hear, resembling the beginning of an earthquake ? It is the sound of the carts bringing merchandise to London. . . . But in the mornings to come there will be less and less travellers to the City, for a reason we shall see. The Plague is approaching London, slow wave by wave, and will overwhelm it like a sea.

Now we, and the carts, are coming nearer to " the noble city of London " (as Andrew Boorde, one of the King's physicians, called it), in that " city which excelleth all others . . . for Constantinople, Venice, Rome, Florence, cannot be compared to London ".

Presently we shall come to the heart of the City, the Tower, and see, fixed to one of the turrets by spears, the skulls " denuded of flesh ", the signs of Henry's vengeance against traitors.

Small dark clouds circling in the sky swoop downwards from time to time, and we see that they are kites and other carrion birds — " so tame ", wrote Trevison, " that they will eat bread and butter out of little children's hands ".

But now we are only on the outskirts — the suburbs which were then the slums and the breeding-places of the Plague, the dwelling-places of the criminal population.

" How happy ", wrote Thomas Dekker, "were cities if they had no Suburbes, sithence they serve but as caves, where monsters are tied up to devoure the Citties their-selves. Would the Divell hire a villain to spil blood ? There we shall finde him. One to blaspheme ? there he hath choice. A Pandar that would court a nation at her praiers ? hees there . . . a cheater that would turne his own father a-begging ? Hees there too. A harlot that would murder her own new-borne Infant ? She lies in there."

Here, the "dores of notorious Carted Bawdes (like Hell-gates) stand night and day wide open, with a paire of Harlots in Taffeta gownes (like two painted posts) garnishing out those dores . . . when the dore of a poore Artificer (if his child had but died with one token of death about him) was close ramm'd up and guarded for feare others should have been infected. Yet the plague a whorehouse lays upon a Citty is worse, yet is laughed at : if not laughed at, yet not look'd into, or if look'd into, wincked at." [4]   And yet " Seriant Carbuncle, one of the Plague's chiefe officers, dare not venture within three yardes of an Harlot, because Mounseer Dry-Bone,* the French-Man, is a Ledger " (lodger) " before him ".[5]

Now we are passing Newington, one of the worst of the slums, and from there move onwards through the shamble-smelling, overhanging streets where the Plague breeds, onward through the streets haunted by Puffing Dick, King of the Beggars, he who " was a man crafty and bold ; yet he died miserably. For, after he had commanded now fully eight years, he had the pyning of the Pox and the Neopolitan scurf, and there was an end of Puffing Dick ".[6]

The company of the beggars, a nation within a nation, living by its own laws, even speaking its own language, was to become, in the reign of Elizabeth, one of the gravest of menaces, till there came a time when that nation bearded, and tried to browbeat, the great Queen in her own person.

By the year 1536, this nation had been joined by the " help-less, needy wretches, unused to dolour, and uninstructed in business " [7] who were turned abroad following the overthrow of the Monasteries. Mr. Ronald Fuller, in *The Beggars' Brother-hood*, gives the number of these condemned to starvation as 88,000.

Every day would see hordes of these poor creatures going to join the company of the ruffians who, at the beginning of Henry's reign, were ruled over by Cocke Lorell, " the thyrde person in the realm " and the terror of the London streets.[8]

* Mounseer Dry-Bone, or syphilis, the appalling disease which, since the capture of Naples by the French in 1495, had ravaged Europe, rivalling and eclipsing leprosy in its horror.

Cocke Lorell may have been a myth, but the later King, Puffing Dick, was a very real personage.

All the old Hospitals, St. Mary Bethlehem, St. Thomas of Southwark, St. Bartholomew, and that terrifying shadow of a nunnery, St. James-in-the-field, " an Hospitall for leprous virgins ", were closed till the end of Henry the Eighth's reign, and their inmates were let loose in the streets, leprous virgins, persons shadowed by Mounseer Dry-Bone, the French-Man, and others.

These lay abroad in the streets of London, mingling their diseases and their miseries, hungry and naked, with wounds coalescing and decomposing under the enormous sun and the freezing moon, their stench offending the passers-by. Sometimes a few of the less helpless would rise up, and in a company of huge trunks, lumps, hulks and hulls, with tatters fluttering like seas, would swarm past the palaces, the monasteries the old occupants of which had gone. If they begged without a written permission, they were rewarded by the pillory, the whip, branding, slavery, or the gallows.

Such was their destitution that they would defy even the Plague. A writer of thirty years later put these words in the mouths of the beggars : " If such plague do ensue, it is no great loss. We beggars reck nought of the carcass, but do defy it ; we look for the old cast coats, jackets, hose, caps, belts and shoes, by their deaths, which in their lives they would not depart from, and this is an hap. God send me one of them. . . ." [9]

Sometimes a roar would echo through the streets from the Bear-garden, that filthy hell where devils from the slums tortured the helpless.

" No sooner was I entered," wrote Thomas Dekker, some sixty years later, " but the very noyse of that place put me in mind of Hell : the beare (dragt to the stake) shewed like a black ragged soule, that was Damned, and newly committed to the infernall Churle, the Dogges like so many Divels inflicting torments upon it.

" At length a blinde Bear was tyed to the stake, and instead of baiting him with dogges, a company of creatures that had the shapes of men, and faces of Christians, (being either Colliers,

Carters, or Watermen) took the office of Beadles upon them, and whipt Mounsier Hunkes, till the blood ran doune his old shoulders : it was some sport to see Innocence triumph over Tyranny, by beholding those unnecessary tormentors go away with scratched hands or torne legs from a porre Beast arm'd only by nature to defend himselfe against Violence : yet methought that this whipping of the blinde Beare moved as much pittie in my breast towards him, as leading of porre starved wretches to the whipping posts in London (when they had need to be relieved with foode) ought to move the Cittizens, though it be the fashion now to laugh at their punishment." [10]

What death could be sufficiently terrible for the tormentors of the starved, I do not know : but one would like to think that those scratched by the blind bear died after suffering the tortures of gangrene. . . . Perhaps they did. . . . I hope so. In any case, we have passed by these chivalrous sports, and the streets, and now move among the airs that drift from the gardens, until we come to a favourite palace of the King, Greenwich, " first builded ", says Harrison in his *Description of England*, " by Humphrie of Gloucester, upon the Thames side foure miles east from London, in the time of Henrie the sixt, and called Pleasance. Afterwards it was greatly enlarged by King Edward IV ; garnished by King Henry VII, and finallie made perfect by King Hen. 8 the arche Phenix of his time for fine and curious masonrie."

This palace of peach-red brick bore everywhere the daisy emblem of Marguerite of Anjou . . . the river ran past it, and the arche Phenix could be rowed in his barge to the steps that led up to the palace. From the mullioned windows the father of the navy could watch his ships as they passed down the river. [11]

As we come nearer, there is a sound of music, approaching us from the direction of the gardens.

NOTES TO CHAPTER ONE

[1] Quoted by J. Dover Wilson, *Shakespeare's England.*
[2] Harrison.
[3] J. Dover Wilson, *Shakespeare's England.*
[4] Thomas Dekker, *The Infection of the Suburbes.*

5 Thomas Middleton, *The Black Booke*.
6 Quoted by Ronald Fuller, *The Beggar's Brotherhood*.
7 *Ibid*.
8 *Ibid*.
9 William Bullein, *A Dialogue against the Pestilence*.
10 Thomas Dekker.
11 See James Pope-Hennessy, *London Fabric*.

Chapter Two

THE voice of trumpets approached — a dark and threatening sound, that seemed as if it heralded the birth of Fate, or told of some great event that would change the history of mankind. Sometimes the musicians came to a bend in the garden path, and then the sound grew distant again, like the whisper of dry leaves or the memory of an old fairy-tale. That sound told the story of a great King whose country was in danger because his male children did not live, of a wicked stepmother — a witch who through her enchantments became Queen, — and of a young disinherited Princess, who, through the spells of her stepmother, became a goosegirl, or a maid to her little sister. Then the sound changed once again, and told of a gigantic tragedy, of a spiritual upheaval in the history of mankind, a Sophoclean drama of an escape from an imagined or pretended incest cursed by heaven : the tale was of bloodshed and of huge lusts of the flesh and the spirit ; of man's desire for spiritual freedom, and of a great Queen who sacrificed her heart and her life on the altar of her country.

The door that led out of the garden opened — and one saw that it was not the birth of Fate that the trumpets proclaimed, but the birth of a child ; a little girl, the centre of this procession. This small red rosebud was the object of all this care and we, with the good and wicked fairies, were invited to the christening.

The procession walked down the garden path strewn with rosemary and green rushes, between the garden walls that have been hung with arras in honour of the event.

" On Sunday last on the eve of Lady Day " (7th September 1533), " about 3 o'clock in the afternoon ", the Imperial Ambassador told the Emperor Charles V, " the King's mistress was delivered of a girl, to the great disappointment and sorrow of the King, of the Lady herself, and of others of her party, and to the great shame and confusion of physicians, astrologers, witches and wizards, all of whom affirmed that it would be a boy. The people in general have rejoiced in the discomfiture of those who attack faith with such divinations. . . .

" It must be concluded that God has entirely abandoned the King, and left him a prey to his own misfortune, and to his obstinate blindness, that he may be punished and completely ruined."

The King's voice was silent now, but since the birth of the child his fury had been terrifying to see and hear : it had raged for three days, breaking from the fires and darkness of his nature. . . . The child a girl ? Was it for this that he had put aside Katherine, his Queen, defied the Emperor and the Pope ?

The astrologers, the physicians, had deceived him. Why, a letter had been prepared which, signed by the new Queen, would announce to the Ministers the birth of a Prince. Now to the word ' Prince ' an S must be added, in the cramped space left for it.

So certain had been the King that heaven was about to grant him his wish for an heir that (wrote the Imperial Ambassador) " he has taken from his treasures one of the richest and most triumphant " (sic) " beds, which was given for the ransome of a Duc d'Alençon. But it was as well for the Lady that it was delivered to her months ago ; for she would not have had it now : because, being full of jealousy, and not without cause, she used words to the King which so displeased him that he told her she must shut her eyes and endure as well as more worthy persons ; and that she ought to know that it was in his power to humble her again in a moment, more than he had exalted her before."

Thomas Dekker, after the death of this being whose christening we are about to witness, wrote — " She came in with the fall of the leafe, and went away in the Springe : her life (which was dedicated to Virginitie) both beginning and closing up in a miraculous Mayden circle : for she was born upon a Lady Eve, and died upon a Lady Eve : her Nativitie and Death being memorable for their wonder ".[1]

Manningham, in his Diary, records that a certain Mr. Rous had said, " The Queen began her raigne in the fall ; and ended

in the spring of the leafe ". " So she did but turne over a leafe ",
said one B. Rudgers.

" The Queen ", wrote Hall, a contemporary historian, " was
delivered of a faire ladye at the noble palace of Greenwich ", so
named, according to Jovius, Bishop of Nocera, " from the
verdure about it ". The room in which the Virgin Queen
was born was named " The Chamber of the Virgins ", because
the tapestries with which it was hung represented the story of
the Wise Virgins ; and when the witch-Queen was told that the
child was not the saviour of England who had been expected
but only a useless girl, she said to the ladies, " They may now,
with reason, call this room the Chamber of the Virgins, for a
virgin is born in it, on the Vigil of the auspicious day in which
the Church commemorates the Nativity of the Virgin Mary ".²

But the King wanted no virgins, blessed or otherwise.
What he needed was a son to succeed him, and to save the
country from civil war.

The bonfires lit in acclamation of the birth, the shouts of the
exultant crowds, were brighter than the fires, louder than the
shrieks, of the martyrdoms that were kindled in vindication of
Henry's regency under God, and in homage to Elizabeth, the
new-born offspring of that almost supreme being. But Henry
knew that the exultation was because of his humiliation, and
that of the witch-Queen, Anne Boleyn. Yet the Te Deum was
sung in honour of the child's birth, and the christening, which
took place on Wednesday the 10th of September, was as magnificent as if the child had indeed been that saviour of England for
whom so much had been dared.

" The Mayor and his brethren," wrote Hall in his *Chronicle*,
" and forty of the chief of the citizens, were commanded to be
at the christening . . . upon the which day the Mayor, Sir
Stephen Pecocke, in a gowne of Crimson Velvet, . . . and all
the Aldermen in Scarlet, with collars and chains, and all the
council of the city with them, tooke their barge after dinner,
at one of the clock . . . and so rowed to Greenwich, where
were many lords, knights and gentlemen assembled. All the
walls between the King's palace and the Friers, were hanged
with arras, and all the way strawed with green Rushes : the

Friers Church was also hanged with Arras.

" The Font was of silver and stood in the midst of the Church, three steps high, which was covered with a fine cloth, and divers gentlemen with aprons, and towels about their necks, gave attendance about it. That no filth should come into the Font, over it hung a square Canopy of crimson Satin fringed with gold. Above it was a rail covered with red silk. Between the choir and the body of the Church, was a close place with a pan of fire, to make the child ready in. When all these things were ordered, the child was brought to the hall, and then every man set forward : First the citizens two and two, then Gentlemen, Esquires and Chaplains, next after them the Aldermen, and the Mayor alone : next the Mayor the King's Council, the King's Chaplain in cope ; then Barons, Bishops, Earls."

The sun of the late summer glittered on the gold cups frosted with pearls, on the gold trains of the company, so that each being seemed a planet in its splendour. But even at the christening of this child of a great fate, the shadow of a triumph brought about by Death was present.

After the long procession of citizens, who were not to be lost to the sunlight, came Henry Bourchier, Earl of Essex, bearing the gilt basons.[3] This magnificent being was the last of his race to bear that title. He was of royal lineage, being descended from Thomas of Woodstock : and to be of royal lineage meant to go through the days and nights in fear. But another fate awaited him from that which he thought watched him from the shade. This " arrogant high hollow fateful rider " was to die, six years after this time, through falling from his horse, and as he had no male heir, his title went from him, and was given by the King to Chief Secretary Cromwell, of the low birth and accommodating conscience.

Next came Henry, Marquis of Dorset, the unfortunate father of Lady Jane Grey. The shadow lay further from him, but it was darker. His eldest daughter was to lose her head because he had plotted to place the Crown upon it. His own life was spared, but only for a while, for shortly after he was to be beheaded because he had taken up arms in the Wyatt rebellion.

He was followed by one whose doom had an equal darkness,

but not an equal splendour — Henry Courtney, Marquis of
Exeter, who carried the taper of virgin wax. This great nobleman had the misfortune to be very near the throne, since his
mother was a daughter of Edward IV. But at this time he
could not see the shade. The King his cousin, after setting aside
his daughter Mary, and his sisters, had declared him heir to the
throne after Elizabeth. But the shade was waiting, was near
him ; although he had not expected it — for it was only a question of which way the light of the sun should fall. In November
1538 Exeter and his wife were sent to the Tower : on the
10th of December he was beheaded ; his estates and honours
were forfeited, and his son, though a child, was imprisoned in
the Tower.

Next came the shy, modest young figure of Lady Mary
Howard, daughter of the Duke of Norfolk, bearing the chrism.
This terrible creature, with the peacefully smiling lips, the head
bent through modesty, was to help bring about the death by
beheading of her own brother, the young Earl of Surrey, the
poet. . . . She was, at the time of the christening, about to
marry the King's bastard son, the young Duke of Richmond,
and after her husband's death this young girl, the familiar friend
of her father's mistress, Bess Holland, for whose sake the half-
mad, termagant Duchess of Norfolk had been discarded, accused
her brother of advising her to try to lure her father-in-law the
King into making her his mistress, in order that she and her
family might gain power over him. This accusation, horrifying
the King, sealed the doom of Surrey, who had already been
attainted for using a version of the royal arms.

The baby Princess, swaddled in a mantle of purple velvet,
with a long train furred with ermine, was carried by one of her
godmothers, the Dowager Duchess of Norfolk, her step-great-
grandmother. On this old woman darkness was to fall through
her part in marrying the guilty Katherine Howard to the King.

The other godmother at the christening was the Dowager
Marchioness of Dorset. Fate was to spare her old head, but
three of her four sons, and her granddaughter Lady Jane Grey,
were to die on the scaffold, and her remaining son was to end
his life as a prisoner, in the reign of Elizabeth, for the fault of

distributing a pamphlet asserting the right of his line to the throne.

The procession advanced, with the first godmother holding the child, the small red rosebud, in the centre. On either side of these walked the Dukes of Norfolk and Suffolk. The fates of these two men were entirely opposite. The Duke of Suffolk, alone among Henry's favourites, kept his favour. Even his marriage to the King's sister Mary, the widowed Queen of France, did not endanger him, but he did not live to see the mournful fates of his younger granddaughters, the children of his daughter Lady Dorset, in the reign of Elizabeth. . . . The Duke of Norfolk, however, was powerful enough to raise Henry's fear that the peace of his own son's reign might be disturbed by the Duke, and no memory of his unvarying fidelity could remove that fear. . . . As the King lay dying, he condemned his old and faithful servant to the scaffold. But then, for the first time, Henry's will was not absolute. The dying King was disobeyed. During the reign of Henry's son, however, the Duke was kept prisoner, to reappear for a short time, restored to his old splendour, in the reign of Mary.

The train of the baby was borne, one one side, by Thomas Boleyn, Earl of Wiltshire, her grandfather : father to a Queen Consort, and grandfather to a future sovereign. But he was to see two of his children, that same Queen Consort, Anne Boleyn, and her brother, Lord Rochford, die on the scaffold. . . .

Of those that carried the canopy, one was that same Lord Rochford, the others were sons of " the illustrious family of Howard, which furnished in this age almost more subjects of tragedy than Thebes and Pelops' line ".

At the door of the church of the Grey Friars, the procession had been received by the Bishop of London, with a great company of Bishops and of mitred abbots. The Bishop of London performed the ceremony of baptism, with all the rites of the Church of Rome. This over, he gave way to Archbishop Cranmer, the child's godfather, who bestowed a solemn benediction. As he stepped forward, the light, for one moment, rested on his face, on the thoughtful, kindly eyes, with their rather plotting expression, the weak mouth and chin. A timid but benevolent man, he was to die among the flames of martyrdom.

But who could have foreseen that such a fate would fall upon one so adaptable and accommodating ? This charming, rather learned, man, of a vacillating will, was forty-three years of age at the time of his royal godchild's christening. " Insinuating and an admirable deceiver ", as Mr. Friedmann said in his *Life of Anne Boleyn*, " who possessed the talent of representing the most infamous deeds in the finest words ", he had, not many months since, risen to be Archbishop, because of his help in the matter of the King's marriage, and perhaps, also, because Chief Secretary Cromwell knew a secret in his life. . . . This priest had broken his vow of celibacy, had gone through a ceremony of marriage with a young woman in Germany. Somehow the matter, secret as it was, had come to the ears of Cromwell's spies. Cranmer's timidity was well known. The slightest act of disobedience, one trace of hesitation to do the bidding of the King and his Minister, and the Archbishop, accused of incontinence, would be deprived and sent to the Tower. . . . A useful servant, and one on whom the King and Cromwell could safely rely.

These were the beings who heralded the fate of Elizabeth. In silence they stood in their appointed places, while the Archbishop's blessing was pronounced. Garter King at Arms cried : " God of His infinite goodness, send a prosperous life and long to the high and mighty, princess of England, ELIZABETH.

" Then the trumpets blew."

The standing cup of gold that was the gift of the Archbishop, the cup of gold frosted over with pearls given by the old Duchess of Norfolk, and the other gifts of gold were presented. " Then wafers, comfits, and ypocras ",* wrote Hall, " were brought in such plenty that every man had as much as he could desire. Then they set forwards, the trumpets going before in the same order, toward the King's place as they did when they came

---

* Mr. Walter de la Mare, in the notes to *Come Hither*, gives this recipe : " To make Hypocras the best way. . . . Take 5 ounces of aqua vitae, 2 ounces of pepper, and 2 of ginger, of cloves and grains of paradice each 2 ounces, ambergrease 3 grains, and of musk 2 grains, infuse them 24 hours in a glass bottle on pretty warm embers and when your occasion requires to use it, put a pound of sugar into a quart of wine or cyder, dissolve it well, and then drop 3 or 4 drops of the infusion, and they will make it taste richly."

thitherward, saving that the gifts that the godfather and the godmothers gave were borne before the child. . . ."

" The shadows haunting faerily the brain ", the beings that seemed planets with their long gold trains like the heat of the sun, would soon be gone. Now, one by one, they moved away in a procession, through the garden door and along the garden path, lighted by the flames of five hundred torches, " borne by the guard and other of the King's servants " into the future.

" In this order ", wrote Hall, " they brought the princess to the Queen's chamber, and the Mayor and the Aldermen tarried there awhile.

" And at last the Dukes of Norfolk and Suffolk came out from the King ; thanking them heartily, and said the King commanded them to give thanks in his name ; and from thence they went to the cellar to drink, and so went to their Barges."

NOTES TO CHAPTER TWO

[1] Thomas Dekker, *The Wonderfull Yeare.*
[2] This story is reported by Leti. I give it for what it is worth.
[3] Lucy Aikin, *Memoirs of the Court of Queen Elizabeh.*

Chapter Three

Falingtado, Falingtado, to wear the black and yellow
Falingtado, Falingtado, my mates are gone : I'll follow.
— *Summer's Last Will and Testament*

THE heavens seemed made of fire, as if the Judgment Day had come, or as if the martyrdoms of the future were prognosticated in the skies — a refulgence spreading like a sea, " the terrible Red Sea of death ", of which Nicholas Sheterden, martyr, wrote to his wife before he was burned " in the sight of God and his angels " ; red and yellow flames of fire changed into seas and lakes of the damned, into the haloes, aureoles, glories of the blessed, or into petals, calyxes, fronds, and vast leaves of flames. These flared upon the horizon, sometimes with a ferine incendiarism, a glare like that of blood, sometimes breaking into a splendour like that of the martyrs' hearts, and of their cries in that death which was to lead to the eternal life — the dying words of John Lambert, " None but Christ — none but Christ " — the cry of a Catholic saint as his heart was torn from his living breast — " What wilt thou do with mine heart, O Christ ? "

Amid the fires of that winter sunset, on the 27th of January 1536, the hollow sound of footsteps echoed through the upper storey of the Queen's apartments in Greenwich Palace. Dying away again, fading to join the dust in remote and unlived-in rooms, the sound of that footfall would soon be forgotten in the high places. But now it came a little nearer to the life in the rooms below.

A young woman was walking downstairs. Slowly she came from the highest storey, turning her head, sometimes, in her descent, as if some voice behind her were urging her on. This was her habit, that from time to time she would look behind her. Sometimes, as she passed a high window, the accusing light fell for a moment on her oval face, with its rather sallow skin, her high broad forehead, her great slanting black eyes, her black hair, and her long throat on which was a mole resembling a strawberry. This was kept hidden by a collar of big pearls, but from time to time she would pull aside the pearls with her left hand, on which was a rudimentary sixth finger. This was a sure sign of a witch, and at the sight of it, whispers arose. It was said that not Lord Wiltshire, but the Prince of the Powers of the Air, was the father of the new Queen.

Step by step she came lower and lower, and with every few steps her aspect seemed to change, according to the direction from which those fires from the skies fell upon her. In the highest storey of all, with the small dazzling notes of an unreal gold falling in showers, in a universal rain, upon her, she seemed a light being, a native of the summer. Then great branches of darkness barred the way, lit by a flare like that of lightning, and she became a creature of the chase, hunter or hunted, who, lost in the forest, had paused for a moment in the desperate flight or pursuit, to listen from which quarter came the sound of the horn. A few steps more ; and a barbarous refulgence fell upon her face, and one could see that she was a place of torment, — not a woman at all ; but an infernal region, a Pandemonium of the Princes of Darkness and all the Powers and Principalities of the Air. Then the darkness of the descent, varying from a Stygian blackness to an umbrageousness like that cast by the boughs of a forest, shrouded her once more, till again the huge fires of the skies, falling through the windows, flaring down on her dress of damned-colour, outlining her body for a moment, made her seem a creature of Doom.

We see her now, as she pauses for an instant on a stair, with the flares casting a light of damnation on her face. So it was that Eustachio Chapuys, the Emperor's Ambassador, saw Anne Boleyn, the Concubine, the pretender Queen. But that face with the light upon it was not the face that her brother, her mother, and the friends to whom she was so faithful, knew.

Is it indeed she, or a creature born of the imagination that we see, as she turns her head to look behind her ?

Great were the changes that the light wrought on this summer being. Yet the extraordinary sense of will-power, of the will to live and to conquer, were such that it seemed as if they must stain the air through which she passed, leaving upon it some colour of summer and its wilfulness, impressing upon the air, for ever, some memory of her being. Then again her face and throat would lie in the blackest shadow, and only her body would be seen — the body of a headless Queen; and you would know that this, too, would soon be enveloped by the waiting darkness, and that all her thoughts and hopes and all that summer existence would soon be forgotten.

She went on her downward way, and as she passed, cold airs drifting through windows, from under the doors of deserted rooms — little rustling airs and the dry whisper of winter leaves blown across a floor, sounded like far-off rumours that would soon come nearer, thickening as they approached, and dry as the dust that would soon engulf her.

Those sounds were almost articulate as they gathered force : " The true Queen had died of a broken heart ". " The Messenger of the King held to her lips a cup." " She drank her death from a cup of gold." " The drink was dark, and it was deep." " Slow was the venom, and insidious." " Some say that the death sank from her throat to her heart." " The poison was sent from Italy by the agent Sir Gregorio da Casale, and was brought to England by his cousin Gurone." " They have given Casale a pension of eight ducats a day, as payment for his part in the work."

Hen voices clacking, feathered voices clucking, adder-voices shrilling and hissing. So sounded the winter airs and the fallen leaves. It is impossible at this time to say how much of truth, how much of falsehood, those voices, those airs, were bringing. The rumours spread over the countryside, for Anne Boleyn was hated and, because of her, the King. The guilty pair were even blamed for the weather. Edmund Brocke, husbandman, eighty years of age, walking home in the rain in August 1535, at Crowle, in Worcestershire, had said to Margaret Higons — " It is 'long of the King that this weather is so troublous and unstable, and I wene that we shall never have better weather whiles the King reigneth, and therefore it makes no matter if he were knocked or patted on the head."—That remark was to bring Mr. Brocke to a death for treason. But still the rumours grew.

Anne Boleyn, walking down the long stairway till she came
to a closed door, opened it, and disappeared into the room
beyond, heedless of rumours or of warning. She had triumphed.
The repudiated wife, the rival Queen, had gone. No longer
would the memory of those eyes, flat, black, blaring yet silent,
and always opened too wide, as if, should she shut them, they
would remain closed for all time, follow, with that inexpressive
gaze, that yet held a continual mockery, the new Queen in her
triumph. Catherine the Queen was dead, and those eyes were
closed for ever. She who had been hunted by the Furies silently,
across the plain of the years, in the heat of the sun, wasted by
the fires in her own nature, clasping her faith to her breast, using
her patience and her virtue as deadly weapons, now lay on her
bier like a dwindled figure of wax that had lain too long exposed
to the heat of the sun.

Yet the triumph of Anne was mixed with a fear — so overwhelming that at times, when she was conscious of it — for it
was not always there, it came and went like the illness which had
destroyed the Queen — Anne would turn cold as if she were
already dead. What would be her own fate, if this second child
she was about to bear was not a son ? . . . Then she would
remember that the Queen was gone, and could trouble her no
more. And with that thought, the chill would pass.

The death of the Queen, delayed, it was thought by many,
through fear of the Emperor Charles the Fifth, her nephew,
had not been undesired, even by those who pretended to be
her protectors. Charles, " void of all excess, either of virtue or
vice, as brave as a prince ought to be, but not as pious as a man
should be ", protected her through pride. But the Pope had
told Stephen Gardiner, the future Bishop of Winchester, that
" it would be for the wealth of Christendom if the Queen
were in her grave " — saying also that " he thought like as the
Emperor had destroyed the temporalities of the Church, so
should she be the destruction of the spiritualities ".[1]

With every day that the life of this saintly yet narrow woman
continued, that life was a menace to the peace of England.
Henry had put her aside mainly in order that he might have a
male heir to the throne. Catherine resisted with all the means

in her power, and although she told Chapuys that she did not ask His Holiness for war, and would rather die than be the cause of it, the conspiracies of the nobles in favour of her and of her daughter, her fears, her prayers to be rescued from the dangers that she believed threatened her, brought the peril of war nearer.

For three years before that time, her fears had increased steadily. Chapuys was warned by some unknown person [2] " to send word to the Queen as soon as possible, that she ought to have her chamber well locked from night till early morning, and carefully examined that none was hidden there, for there was a danger that they should play some trick upon her, either an injury to her person, or an accusation of adultery, or a charge of plotting to go to Scotland or Wales and raise an insurrection ".

The Queen feared that her death would follow, and with equal tortures, the martyrdom of those gentle saints the Monks of the Charterhouse, whose hearts were torn from their bodies because they defied Henry's will, in refusing to take the oath of allegiance to Anne and her offspring as Queen and heir to the throne, and to Henry as Supreme Head of the Church.

But martyrdom was not the only fate that the Queen believed threatened her.

Nothing seemed to her safe. Even when the King and Secretary Cromwell showed her an apparent amiability, she feared that this hid some new danger. She told the Emperor, " I cannot forbear to tell you that I am as Job, waiting for the day when I must sue for alms for the love of God."

For the King was often slow in paying the moneys due to her.

Yet Henry's generosities were great, and the Privy Purse expenses record sums of money paid to " An old Poor Man, that laboured to obtain a bill to be signed ", to " a footman to relieve him in his sickness ", " to little Gwilliam, because he was sick in London ", " to a blind man being a harper ", " to a frantick man ", to " a poor woman labouring to obtain her husband's freedom and hers in London ".[3]

" These gifts ", wrote the editor of the *Privy Accounts*, " could only have emanated from momentary motions of benevolence, and they prove that, like even greater monsters, Henry's heart was not entirely shut to the wants and sufferings of his fellow creatures."

To Catherine's they were shut, for the moment, because she had opposed that princely will, and because it was no question of generosity, but of giving her what was rightfully hers.

Under this rain of complaints, Chapuys urged the Emperor to consider invading England, to avenge "the enormous injury done to your Aunt. The enterprise", he wrote, " would be more justifiable to obviate the scandal which will arise from the divorce, and likewise to prevent the kingdom from alienating itself entirely from the Holy Father ". This was in 1533.

Everywhere the country was ripe for rebellion. Bishop Fisher had urged the Emperor to invade England, seconded in this advice by the young Marquis of Exeter. The discontented among the lords were listening to the half-fraudulent, half-mad, falsely-illuminated Nun of Kent, Elizabeth Barton, as she prophesied death to the King and woe to his new marriage. It was said everywhere that the King, by his sins, had forfeited the crown and that his death, either by visitation of God or by visitation of man, was imminent. Was there not a northern prophecy that " the decorate Rose should be slain in his mother's belly " . . . and did this not mean, as certain of the friars believed, that the King would die by the hands of priests ? . . .

Such were the conditions in England when, in December 1533, three months after the birth of Elizabeth, Chapuys assured the Emperor that people would be glad to see the Emperor's fleet, and that many declared he had a better title to be King of England than the monarch who reigned.

" If you do not claim the title," he continued, "they " (certain discontented nobles) " think that forbidding intercourse with Flanders is the best course. The King is very much afraid of that, knowing he could not prevent a mutiny unless he were willing for some time to subsidise those who live by making cloth, who are considerably more than half the people of England; and this he could not do without double the money he has. Though this would make him popular, I think the sin into which he has fallen will not allow him to do it, or anything else that he ought to do."

The King's gigantic strength of will and of nature prevented the dangers of war and of rebellion from becoming facts. But they increased as time went on, and at last were only averted by the death of the Queen.

Chief Secretary Cromwell began to throw out hints about the benefits that would arise from the deaths of the Queen and the Princess. These were countered by veiled threats from the Emperor's Ambassador as to what might happen should those deaths occur.

On the 30th of June 1535, he told the Emperor that Cromwell had said, " If God had taken to himself the Queen and the Princess, the whole dispute " (between the King and the Pope) " would have been ended, and no one would have doubted or opposed the King's second marriage, or disputed the Succession, unless it were the King of Scotland, of whom he made no great account."

The Ambassador's reply had a sinister tone. In a gentle voice he said he thought there were others who might make claims . . . oh, not the Emperor ! His Imperial Majesty was not so ambitious. But what would happen were the Pope to fulminate censures and invoke the aid of the secular arm to deprive the King of his titles and deliver his kingdom to whoever might take possession of it ? Would not this be the most Catholic title any prince could have ?

Cromwell was silent for a moment. Then he replied that the Emperor was bound by so many treaties to King Henry that it was unbelievable that they could be broken.

But his voice had a hollow sound.

. . . The death of an old, unwanted woman . . . so small a flame to be extinguished. . . .

And the choice lay between that or rebellion. . . .

Cromwell asked himself if Chapuys really believed he knew nothing of what was going on — was ignorant of Chapuys' secret conversations with the malcontent lords — his ponderings as to whether it would be better to marry the Princess to the King of Scotland and dethrone her father that they might take his place, to marry her to some great English noble and raise an internal rebellion, or to do as Catherine suggested, choose

Reginald Pole, grandson of the Duke of Clarence, as Mary's husband, since he already had claims to the throne.

The veiled threats against the life of Catherine continued.

Three years before the death of the Queen, Gregorio da Casale, the agent sent by Henry to the Pope, whispered to Chapuys that the King had grave doubts if Catherine, who had been his Queen, would live long. She had a dropsy, he said.

The Ambassador replied sternly that the Queen had never suffered from dropsy. But he knew, or thought that he knew, the meaning that lay behind the rumour. This illness was to be induced in her by artificial means, or she would die by some subtle poison which would produce the symptoms of dropsy. Anne, the supplanter-Queen, had laid her plans, as she believed, in secrecy. But Dr. Ortiz warned the Emperor two days after the birth of Elizabeth (9th September 1533) that he had been told in Rome by the auditor Simonetti that Anne purposed the Queen's death and that she had become openly threatening. In the summer of 1534, a conversation was overheard between the witch-Queen and her brother Lord Rochford in which she said that when the King was in France and she was his Regent, she would have Mary executed for disobedience. Rochford warned her of the King's rage, but she replied, violently, that she would do it even if she were burned or skinned alive as a punishment.

Later, Dr. Ortiz, visiting England in the Imperial service, told his master (22nd November 1535) that "La Mancheba" (Anne) had often said of Mary, " She is my death, and I am hers, so I will take good care that she shall not laugh at me after my death."

By this time, the threats, from being veiled, had suddenly become open and immediate : the danger was very close.

On the 6th of November, the Marchioness of Exeter, a devoted adherent of the Queen, warned Chapuys that the King had lately told his most trusted councillors that he would no longer remain in this trouble, fear, and suspicion on account of the Queen and Princess. This he swore with great oaths.

A fortnight later, according to the same informant, Henry swore that he would contrive that Mary should need neither New Year's gifts nor company. She should be made an example to all that no one could disobey the law with impunity.

But the King's councillors heard these threats with fear. They knew a Bill of Attainder against the Queen and Princess would be followed instantly by an uprising backed by the power of the Emperor. Not only would the King be in danger ; but also the properties and lives of those who were his Ministers.

The King's threat was uttered in November . . . and was listened to in silence by the Council. Four weeks later the illness of the Queen began.

Was that illness encompassed, or did she die, as modern authorities have thought, of melanotic sarcoma, the cancer of the heart ? At the time of her death, the rumour spread over Europe that she was poisoned. The Emperor believed it, Chapuys was convinced of it ; and at the trial of Anne Boleyn, a scapegoat having been found, this charge was brought against her.

The Imperial Ambassador told his master, when he heard of the Queen's death, " Should they open her, the traces will be seen. . . ."

Catherine died, at two o'clock in the afternoon, of that mysterious illness that came, and went for a little, leaving a shadow upon her face, leaving the waxen figure a little more shrunken, more twisted, and then returned again, and remained, and would not go until the being it haunted lay dead.

" January the 7th," wrote Sir Edward Bedingfield, Keeper of the house where the Queen passed her nun-like existence, " about ten o'clock the lady dowager was aneled with the holy ointment ; master chamberlain and I being called to the same, and before two in the afternoon she departed to God. I beseech you that the King may be advised of the same."

It was a cold day in January, but the keepers of the house where she lay decided that the woman who had died at two o'clock must be embalmed the same night, by the house-chandler, and enclosed in lead, far from the eyes of men — " the which ", he wrote to Secretary Cromwell, " must soon be done, for the work will not tarry ".

Why would the work not tarry, on this cold day of January ? The silent creature to whom that note was written may have known of a reason. It is not only the heat of the sun that brings corruption.

The work must be done quickly, as if the fires of the sun that flare over the dead woman's native Granada, were at their height. So at ten o'clock that night, the dead Queen's confessor, Juan de Atequa, the old Spanish Bishop of Llandaff, her doctor Miguel de la Sà, and her apothecary de Soto, were told they must quit the room where she lay, leaving the chandler of the house and his two assistants alone with the body.

Surrounded by the yellow flares of great candles, the waxen figure that had been wasted by fires lay on her bier, under a black-velvet pall embossed with a large silver cross and the royal escutcheon of Spain.

In the yellow flickering light of the candles, the shadows of the three men who must leave their Queen on her death-bed, were thrown upon the wall — black shadows with exaggeratedly long noses like those of Punchinello. One shadow stooped a little, as if it had been eavesdropping. Dr. de la Sà, for months past, had seemed to be listening — in the house, in the gardens — for something unheard by the rest of the world. He seemed always, now, to be about to tell a secret, bending towards his companions, warningly, as if to enjoin them to silence. . . . He, the Queen's confessor and the apothecary, left the room.

In the early morning, finding those faithful servants of the dead woman waiting, alone, in the anteroom, the chandler and his two assistants told them, in a fearful undertone (as though the words they said, if repeated, would cost them their lives), that at first they had thought the body of the dead Queen was quite sound. Then they saw the heart, which lay exposed in the opened breast. That heart, exposed to their eyes and to the light of the candles, was entirely black, and hideous to the sight.

They stood staring at it for a moment, in silence. Then they washed the heart, strongly, in water that they changed three times. But that frightful blackness did not alter. Seeing this, the chandler clove the heart in two, and found its innermost depths were of the same blackness that no water could wash away.

This was the secret that they whispered to the Queen's devoted servants. Then, looking at them with terror, the chandler and

C

his assistants told them they had found a black thing, clinging to the core of the heart with such force that it could not be dislodged.

That black heart and the body it had consumed as a fire melts wax, were shut away in a covering of lead before the light of day could witness the fate that had befallen them.

Next day, came the mourners who were to watch beside the body and follow in the funeral procession — the young Duchess of Suffolk, the Countess of Worcester, the young Countess of Bedford, and a number of other ladies. The Queen lay, night after night, amid the banners proclaiming her great lineage — the houses of Aragon, Castile, Sicily, Naples, Portugal, the Empire, and with these, the banners of Lancaster, of England, four great standards of gold, on one of which was painted the Trinity, on another Our Lady, on the third St. Katherine, and on the fourth St. George — little pennons on which were portrayed the device of King Ferdinand, father of the deceased, and the device of the dead Queen, with other banners bearing the painted emblems of the bundle of arrows, the pomegranate, the lion, the greyhound. And round the chapel were painted in letters of gold the words " Humble et Loyal ".

On the night when the funeral procession arrived at Peterborough Cathedral, a dirge was sung. Next morning the three funeral masses were celebrated, and the nine chief mourners made offerings of cloth of gold. But the dead woman went to her grave under the title, not of Queen, but of Princess Dowager. Therefore her old and faithful friend the Imperial Ambassador did not attend the funeral of " her who for twenty-seven years has been true Queen of England, whose holy soul, as every one must believe, is in eternal rest, after worldly misery borne by her with such patience that there is little need to pray for her ".

The fires in her heart were gone. But they had faded slowly. And sometimes, as though the heat of those fires had melted the heart itself into rain, that could only find release in weeping, the stones on which she knelt in prayer were wet with her tears. As she lay dying, she who had said " it were better to be judged in Hell, for no truth can be suffered here, whereas the devils themselves I suppose do tremble to see the truth in this cause

so far offended ", sent to her husband a letter which her own hand
was too weak to write :

" My lord and dear husband, — I commend me unto you,
the hour of my death draweth fast on, and my case being such,
the tender love I owe you forceth me with a few words to put
you in remembrance of the health and safeguard of your soul,
which you ought to prefer before any consideration of the
world or flesh whatsoever, for which you have cast me into
many miseries and yourself into many cares. For my part I do
pardon you all : yes, I do wish and dearly pray God that he
will also pardon you. For the rest, I commend unto you Mary
our daughter, beseeching you to be a good father unto her, as
I have hitherto desired. I entreat you also on behalf of my maids,
to give them their marriage portions, which is not much, they
being but three. For all my other servants, I solicit a year's pay
more than their due, lest they should be unprovided for. Lastly,
I vow that mine eyes desire you above all things.
  " Farewell."

Perhaps as she lay dying, Catherine saw the only man she
had loved as he was in his youth. But he was changed, to her,
and to all men : the prince with the face of an angel who had
fallen under the spell of his own princely will.

Wolsey, who understood Henry better than any of his other
Ministers, said, on his death-bed, " He is sure a prince of royal
courage, and hath a princely heart ; and rather than he will
either miss or want any part of his will or appetite, he will put
the loss of one half of his realm in danger. For I assure you
that I have often kneeled before him in his privy chamber on
my knees the space of an hour or two, to persuade him from
his will and appetite ; but I could never bring it to pass to
dissuade him therefrom. . . . Therefore . . . I warn you to be
well advised and assured what matter ye put into his head, for
ye shall never put it out again."

With Catherine's death, an obstacle in the path of that
princely will had been removed.

Therefore, in answer to that letter from the tomb, the Court rang with the noise of balls and feasts. The King exclaimed, " God be praised that we are free from all danger of war." And the father and brother of Anne, openly exulting, declared that the only thing they regretted was that the Lady Mary was not keeping her mother company.

The King and his new Queen both wore yellow — for mourning, as it was said.

The day after the death was a Sunday, and the usurper-Queen's child was carried, with great pomp, preceded by trumpets and followed by a train of servants, to Mass. In the afternoon was a Court ball, and the husband of the dead woman, " clad all in yellow from top to toe, excepting for the white feather he had in his bonnet ", entered the room where the ladies were dancing and there did several things like as one transported with joy. At last he sent for his little Bastard, and carrying her in his arms, he showed her first to one and then to another." [4]

Watching the little child, leaping up and down in her father's arms, where the great fires lit the winter dusk, who could imagine this being as she would be in sixty-five years' time — the old sandalwood body smelling of death, the beautiful hands that were like long leaves, grown a little dry from age, so that the lines on the palms were like those on a map ? Then, too, she would leap into the air like a thin flame — like the flames she saw as she was about to die. (" I saw one night ", she told one of her ladies, " my body exceeding lean and fearful in a light of fire.")

In those last days of her life she danced to the sound of a pipe and a drum, alone, in a small room, excepting for the musicians and her faithful friend and lady-in-waiting Lady Warwick. She danced, as she did everything, to fight the shadow of death. When she could no longer dance, she would sit and watch the maids of honour dancing — to the sound of the Dargason or Sedany, Flaunting Two (a country dance), Mopsy's Tune, Turkerloney, Frisks, the Bishop of Chester's Jig, the Spanish Lady, Farnaby's Woodycock, Nobody's Jig, Dusty, my Dear — and perhaps the wonderful Lachrymae Pavanes of Dowland, published in 1605, three years after her death, with a number of other Pavanes, Galliards, and Almands, in a book with the title *Lachrimae, or Seaven Teares, figured in Seven Passionate Pavanes,* — the last words being

Happy, happy they that in Hell feel not the world's despite.

But now she, a little child, who knew nothing of that despite, is singing in imitation of the music.

Yet even now she was the heroine of a triumph brought about by death — that of her mother's rival. To her mother, and to many others, her birth had been like the birth of Fate. The fires and the rivers of blood of the martyrdoms, the death of the old order, heralded her coming ; and, from her first cry, Death followed her everywhere. Sometimes it would seem only a shadow in the heat of the day. She would be playing, perhaps — and there would be Death, waiting quietly. Or Death's voice would sound through the lips of people she knew, or, still more, through their silence. Soon, when she was old enough to speak, she would ask, " Has the Queen my mother gone away ? " But that would not be yet, for there were still four months between this time and the day of her mother's beheading — and then Elizabeth would not be three years old. " Where is she ? at Hampton Court ? " . . . Silence. Then Death would come again. Her stepmother, Queen Jane, would vanish, and could not be found in the great staterooms or in the unoccupied rooms of the Palace. " The Queen's grace is dead." " Why did she die ? " " She died when the Prince's grace was born." Then that later stepmother, the lewd, sly, pitiable little ghost Katherine Howard, who came back to haunt the King from the tomb of her cousin, Elizabeth's mother — she too would vanish. " Why has she gone away ? " " The King's grace was angered against her. She is dead." " *Dead ?* " " Yes, the King's grace has had her put to death because she was wicked."

Thus the word Death echoed through the Palace.

The various fates of these three women were to alter the whole of Elizabeth's life, coming, as they did, at the most impressionable ages of her childhood : they were to affect her sexually, laying the chill of death on her hot blood, in the midst of passion ; they were to instil moments of cold fear into the veins of this lion-brave creature. But that was to come : now Elizabeth is a little child, clapping her hands at the sound of the trumpets and the triumph, and because she saw everyone laughing.

The balls, the joustings, continued.

But on the 24th of the month, the King fell from his horse. . . . He was unhurt, but the fall seemed to him a warning, — perhaps of the wrath to come. The gaiety, the rejoicings, stopped. Darkness fell. But not before Henry had instructed his Ambassador in France to point out to Francis I that, Catherine being dead, there was no longer any need for the King of England to fear the hostility of the Emperor. The French King might find himself forestalled, if he did not immediately accept the proposals of the King of England — and by the Emperor Charles, the nephew of the dead woman whose plaints could no longer disturb the peace of Europe.

NOTES TO CHAPTER THREE

[1] Gardiner to the King.
[2] Letter from Chapuys to the Emperor Charles V, December 27, 1535.
[3] *Privy Accounts : Henry VIII.*
[4] Chapuys to the Emperor.

Chapter Four

THE beings of this Sophoclean tragedy of passions, faiths, lusts, and ambition that had the fever of lust, poured out their blood and spirit in a world of giant spiritual upheavals. Henry the King, once beautiful for all his monstrousness, half a bestial bulk of physical matter, half a kingly being of enlightened greatness and primitive intellect, Catherine, the deserted Queen, a dark and sombre Niobe weeping for her children, and Anne, the summer lightning — these, their forms, their actions, were lit by the enormous flares of fires in which the martyrs perished, kindled in vindication of Henry's regency under God, and in homage to Elizabeth, the new-born offspring of that almost supreme being. Those flares show a face of kingly power, marred by passions and self-will, the face of a darkened and burnt-out Queen-nun, and a face of unutterable terror ; a laughing mouth and tears falling like comets down a face that held all the summer's beauty. We think that a voice is about to speak — then a thunderous darkness falls again, and a faint sound arises — the whispering of plots, like the crepitating sound that comes before an earthquake.

The scene, the events, and the beings of the tragedy were bound together in such a manner as to be indivisible. The tragedy had grown slowly and inevitably from the character of the time, and of the actors, from the change in the minds of mankind, from an imaginary incest, superstitious fear, the King's overwhelming infatuation, his lust for power, his need for a son who would save his kingdom from the danger of civil war.

"If ever ", wrote the Reverend Father, Herbert Thurston, S.J., in the *Catholic Encyclopedia,* "a moral and religious cataclysm was the work of one man, most assuredly the first stage in the Reformation in England was the work of Henry VIII. The new learning," he continues, "the humanism of scholars, the discovery of America, had fired the imagination."

Fate had chosen a great, even at times an illuminated character,

31

" of whom, one would say ", wrote Erasmus, " that he was a universal genius ", and a darkened and evil, but yet great man, Wolsey, as the pre-ordained actors in this side of the drama. Henry, that tragic and lonely being, a giant in scale, a creature of powerful intellect and insane pride, of cruelty, vengeance, and appalling rages, of kingly generosity and breadth of understanding, of half-lies and half-truths, a great King in the primitive sense, a human being of such unsurpassable, irresistible charm that we feel it even at this distance of time, had helped to bring about the tragedy through two factors, his kingly sense of duty to his people, and his curious power of self-deception.

He has been much misjudged : Charles II has been forgiven for his lusts and pruriencies because he, and they, were little and nasty, and littleness is understood and sympathised with by petty people. Henry, whose morality was higher, in spite of the plague that destroyed him, has never been forgiven for his six marriages, because he was a being of elemental greatness, and this alien quality creates hatred.

Henry had inherited a strong religious strain. In youth, he had earned from Pope Leo X the title of Defender of the Faith, by his vindication against Luther of the Catholic doctrine. " He is very religious ", wrote Giustinian,[1] " and hears three masses daily when he hunts, and sometimes five and six on the other days. He hears the office every day in the Queen's " (Catherine's) " chamber — that is to say Vespers and Compline." The most eminent theologians and doctors were regularly required to preach at Court, and Erasmus declared that the Court was an example to all Christendom for learning.

But that learning, that zeal, and above all, the King's conscience, made him more dangerous.

Never were savagery and benevolence more strangely mixed in a nature. " Tolerance and clemency were no small part of his character in early manhood ", wrote Professor A. F. Pollard ; " his influence on his people was enlightened." " In short " (as Chieregati told Isabella d' Este in 1517) " the wealth and civilisation of the world are here ; and those who call the English barbarians, appear to me to render themselves such. I here perceive very elegant manners, extreme decorum, and very great politeness. And amongst other things, there is this most invincible King, whose accomplishments and qualities are so many and excellent that I consider him to surpass all who ever wore a crown : and blessed and happy may this country call itself in having as its lord so worthy and eminent a sovereign, whose sway is more bland and gentle than the greatest liberty under any other."

But Henry's violent obstinacy was the ruling quality of his life. This Minotaur who could, as Catherine had said, " be driven like a bull into the arena ", could only be so driven when he believed his own will to be the motive power. And yet, he would listen patiently to a Minister, and, though he pursued his own way, he never punished or disgraced a counsellor whose views were not his own.

In his youth, there was nobody to combat that royal will, and when, with his wish to set aside Catherine of Aragon, that will was crossed for the first time, he succeeded in persuading himself that he had committed a crime against God and man in marrying the widow of his brother, that he was incestuous and must suffer as a Divine punishment the death of his children by Catherine. It was in order, he told himself, to escape from his sin that he wished the marriage to be declared null. " For if a man shall take his brother's wife, it is an unclean thing. They shall be childless." . . . So said the Book of Deuteronomy. The King knew — or we believe he knew — that the Queen's marriage with his brother had been in name only. But he set the thought aside. He remembered only that he had defied God's commandment and that God's regent on earth, by reason of his semi-Divine kingship, was yet accursed by God because of his sin.

In this belief, he began to hate the blinded partner of his guilt, feeling a spiritual and physical horror in her presence, knowing that not only he, the incestuous King, but his people, were doomed by this curse from Heaven, since only by the birth of a male heir to the throne could civil war be averted from England.

His marriage to Anne Boleyn was, in fact, an incest, since Mary Boleyn, her sister, had been his mistress. It was even whispered of him that a far more frightful crime had been committed by him in marrying Anne, — that he had been the lover of her mother, Lady Elizabeth Boleyn. In this last calumny there is no shadow of truth. The former story is true, but there is this difference between the two incests : Henry believed that by his marriage with Catherine he had injured the memory of his dead brother, and had committed a deadly sin against the royal line of England — whereas by marrying Anne after having been the lover of her sister, he had injured no one.

One by one, Fate struck down all the beings who stood near this tragedy, as if they lived in an infected air. And in each case the doom was the inevitable punishment of the victim's own sin.

Henry sent his second wife to the scaffold, and we shall never know the truth — whether she was innocent or guilty — whether Henry believed in her fault or blinded himself to her innocence because he wished her out of his way. Everything connected with that tragedy is covered by darkness and dust. The present writer thinks that Henry believed her guilty, but that she was not so : in fact after the death of Anne Boleyn, Chapuys was told by one of Henry's gentlemen that the King had refused the hand of Francis the First's daughter, " because she was too young, and for the reason ' qu'il avait trop expérimenté avec la dicte Concubine que cestoit de la pourriture de France ' ".[2]

It is possible, though highly improbable, that Anne, in her terror at finding herself unable to give birth to a male child by the King, may have tried to produce, by means of a sin, an heir to the kingdom, in order to save her own life, which she believed to be threatened by that failure. But against this, there is her oath, taken as she was about to die, that she was innocent. Would she (for she was not devoid of faith) have risked damnation by calling God to witness what was a lie, and by dying with that lie upon her lips ?

We know this alone, that Anne was guilty towards Catherine, although it is improbable that she contrived her death by poison. And that whether Henry was, or was not, guilty towards his second wife, there crept out of her blood-stained grave a horrible yet pitiable little ghost, Katherine Howard, the dead woman's cousin, with an apeish lewdness and lust that seemed the phantom, suddenly turned real, of the sin for which Anne had suffered, and which may, or may not, have existed only in the mind of Henry. And that ghost struck him down. From that moment, he was an old man waiting for death.

Cardinal Wolsey had plotted the overthrow of Catherine, the true Queen. He was brought to his destruction, not by her hand, but through the plots of the woman who was the instrument of her ruin — though not the instrument he had chosen — (he wished Henry to marry the daughter of the French King). Anne Boleyn plotted to take the place of the Queen whose maid of honour she had been. She went to her death largely, it is supposed, through the plots of her own maid of honour, or that maid's supporters. Jane Seymour, the woman in question, connived, possibly, at the death of Anne, in order that she might become Queen and give the King a son. She died as a result of giving birth to that son. Cromwell was to suffer death, some years later, as a result of his own practice. He had grown used to flattering. But he said what he thought would be pleasing to his master, once too often. He was careless once only, but his balance was precarious on the high path to which he had climbed, and he fell. Then he who had introduced the infamous law of condemnation by attainder without trial, in the case of the Countess of Salisbury, was the first to die according to it. He suffered death before the old woman whose end he had encompassed.

Such were the beings who helped bring about an upheaval in the spiritual history of mankind.

But above all, that upheaval was brought about by the King's need of an heir.

The Cardinal Governor of Bologna declared that ". . . if the King should die without heirs male, he was sure it would cost two hundred thousand men's lives ". . . . At one time " Even his Holiness ", Gardiner told Wolsey, " began to reckon what titles might be pretended by the King of Scots and others, and granted that without an heir male . . . the realm was like to come to dissolution ". Catherine's children were either born dead, or died within two months of their birth —

with one exception, that of Mary.

On the 31st of January 1510, seven months after the marriage, a dead child, a daughter, was born. Then, on the 1st of January 1511, came the heir to the throne. He lived until the 22nd of February, when, having caught cold at his christening, the little creature died. In September 1513, according to the Venetian Ambassador,[3] Catherine gave birth to another son, who was either born dead or who died immediately after birth. In June 1514, there was again a mention of the King's new son, and his christening : he, too, died soon after the ceremony. Then we find Henry taunting Catherine with her father's treachery, and with his own conquests ; and to this brutality, says Dr. Pollard, Martyr attributes the premature birth of Catherine's fourth son, towards the end of 1514. According to a Venetian writing from Rome, as early as August 1514, there was a rumour "that the King of England means to repudiate his present wife, the daughter of the King of Spain".[4] But then Mary was born, on the 18th of February 1516, and, for the time being, there was no more mention of a divorce. It was said the Queen was about to bear another child, in August 1517, but then there is silence, and it is probable that she had several miscarriages at about this time. On the 10th of November 1518, there was yet another still-born child. In 1519 " the King swore that he would lead a crusade in person if he should have an heir".[5] But no doctors — either the English or those sent from Spain — were of any avail. By 1525 the last hope was dead. Henry was then but thirty-four. . . . Of his marriage wrote the French Ambassador in 1528, " God has long ago passed sentence on it ".[6]

But the Emperor and his will stood in the way of the King's remarriage, and the Pope was in great fear.

" Of the three great temporal Potentates in Europe," wrote Dr. Pollard,[7] " Charles was the most powerful. For he ruled Castille and Aragon, the Netherlands, Naples, Burgundy and Austria . . . he could command the finest infantry in Spain, the science of Italy, the lance-knights of Germany were at his disposal, and the wealth of the Indies was poured out at his feet. He bestrode the narrow world like a Colossus, and the only hope of lesser men lay in the maintenance of Francis' power. Were that to fall, Charles would become arbiter of Christendom, Italy a Spanish kingdom, and the Pope little more than the Emperor's chaplain."

Since the Sack of Rome in 1527, the Pope was virtually the Emperor's prisoner. He had been elected Pope by Imperial influence, and even before the Sack of Rome was thought to be the Emperor's creature. "Great masters", said Turnstall, with reference to a papal brief urged by Charles, "could get great clerks to say what they liked. . . . If the great clerk were called upon to decide between the great master and Henry, it was obvious that all Henry's service to the Papacy would count for nothing."

If, as Froude has said,[8] " the Pope decided for Henry, he lost Germany, if for Catherine, while Henry was supported by Francis, France and England threatened both to fall from him. . . . Francis cared nothing for the question at stake, his aim was to make the breach between Henry and the Emperor, his great rival, irreparable, and by inducing the Pope to consent to the King's demands, to detach the See of Rome conclusively from the imperial interests. . . . The Pope's only cause, therefore, was to induce the Emperor to show patience, while he worked upon the King of France ; and if France and England could once be separated, he trusted they would yield in despair."

The Pope had not a character fitted to deal with great events. " He was very reserved,[9] irresolute, and decides few things for himself. He loves money and prefers persons who know where to find it to any other kind of men. He likes to give himself the appearance of being independent, but the result shows that he is generally governed by others." " The Pope ", the same writer told Charles V, " is at the disposal of the conqueror."

Over the question of the annulment of Henry's marriage, Clement the Fifth, that predatory creature, with the narrow face, and lips drawn up close under the snuffling, long nostrils — a mask that was lupine or vulpine, according to the light in which it was seen, temporised. He wept, when he believed that his tears were not watched, he wrung his hands. Sometimes, he hinted he would allow the settlement of " the King's question ". At other moments he fulminated threats. " He has told me three

times in secret ", wrote the Bishop of Tarbes to Francis (27th
March 1531), " that he would be glad if the marriage " (with
Anne Boleyn) " was already made, either by dispensation of the
English legate or otherwise, provided it was not by his authority
or in diminution of his power as to dispensation and limitation
of Divine Laws." . . .

On the 18th of September in the same year, the agent Casale
informed the King that " a few days since, the Pope secretly
proposed to me that your Majesty might be allowed two wives.
I told him I could not undertake to make any such proposition,
because I did not know whether it would satisfy your Majesty's
conscience. I made this answer, because I know that the Im-
perialists have this in view, and are urging it; but why, I
know not."

The same thought had struck the King, who, unknown to
Wolsey, sent his secretary Dr. Knight on a Commission to
Rome to put the suggestion before His Holiness; but for some
reason the Commission was withdrawn before the journey was
accomplished.

And still the Pope, though he wept and wrung his hands,
was no nearer to settling the question. His threats became more
frequent.

When it became clear that nothing was to be expected from
him, Anne urged the King not to wait for the dissolution of his
marriage with Catherine, but to marry her — Anne — immediately. But the King replied only that for her sake he had made
many enemies. " What does that matter," she cried — how
could that be compared with the fact that she had braved all
for his sake — even the ancient prophecies that a Queen of
England would be burned alive at this time. Even if she must
die a thousand deaths, it would abate nothing of her love.[10]

At last, in order that he might have his own way, and in
order that he might produce the saviour of England, Henry
braved the risk of excommunication, that final seal of eternal
damnation.

NOTES TO CHAPTER FOUR

[1] *Venetian Calendar*, i. 1287.

[2] Chapuys to N. de Granvelle, June 6, 1538, *Vienna Archives*, 229½, iii. Fol. 12 ; Paul Friedmann, *Life of Anne Boleyn*.

[3] *Venetian Calendar*, ii. 329.

[4] *Ibid.* ii. 479.

[5] A. F. Pollard, *Henry VIII*.

[6] Du Bellay to Montmorence, November 1, 1528, quoted by A. F. Pollard, *op. cit.*

[7] A. F. Pollard, *Henry VIII*.

[8] Froude, *Henry VIII*.

[9] Sessa, quoted by A. F. Pollard, *op. cit.*

[10] Chapuys to Charles V, July 11, 1530. *Vienna Archives*, P.C. 226.F, Fol. 59.

Chapter Five

ANNE BOLEYN became the King's mistress, it is supposed, in September 1532, when she was created Marchioness of Pembroke. A marriage between them took place, in secret, except for a handful of people, on the morning of the 25th of January 1533, very early, before it was light. It is not certain what priest was found " so servile and so perjured " [1] as to perform the ceremony ; but Chapuys believed this man to have been an Augustinian friar, afterwards made General of the Mendicant Friars.

On the 9th of March, before the marriage was known, the King and his new Queen went to hear a sermon, the burden of which was that Henry, so long as he had lived with Catherine, had been in a state of deadly sin, and that he was bound now to marry a virtuous woman, though she might be of lesser birth.

Their church-going had not always been so happy. On the 1st of May 1532, Father (afterwards Cardinal) Peto, preaching at Greenwich in the King's presence, on the text " Where the dogs licked the blood of Naboth, even there shall they lick thy blood, O King ", turned directly to Henry with these words, " And now, O King, hear what I say to thee, I am that Micaiah whom thou wilt hate, because I tell thee truly that this marriage is unlawful. . . . Take heed lest thou, being seduced, find Ahab's punishment, who had his blood licked up by the dogs."

Henry left the chapel without showing any sign that he had heard.

Anne Boleyn appeared for the first time as Queen nearly three months after that secret marriage — on Saturday the 12th of April 1533. On that day of her open triumph, trumpets preceded her, and her train was borne by the Duchess of Richmond.

With that marriage, that triumph, the fate of Anne Boleyn began its dark downward course : they were but the beginning of her death.

Catherine the Queen, with her sombre nobility, her narrow-

ness, her occasional sourness, her inability to bear the King a
son who would live beyond a few weeks, and the other woman
with her summer lightness, the woman who was young and
would surely bear him a son — these were but symbols in this
war for the future of England. — But Anne Boleyn saw herself
as more than that — as a necessity to the King, as a part of his
life. Was it not for her sake that he had entered into a spiritual
war with the Pope ? He had even sent Ambassadors to the
King of Scotland, in an attempt to persuade him to withdraw
his obedience from the Apostolic See. But as the Ambassadors
" entered upon their heresies, there arose a gigantic thunder "
and, in this eclipse of the light, this Cimmerian blackness alter-
nating with even more appalling sheets and torrents of lightning,
the King of Scotland made the sign of the Cross — not so much,
he explained, for fear of the thunder as in horror at the Ambassadors' impious suggestions.

Contrasted with Catherine's wintry darkness and narrowness,
Anne had seemed to Henry a part of the summer, a garden wife,
" a wife with a strawberry breath, cherry lips, apricot cheeks,
and a soft velvet head like a melicotton ".

But only for a while. What he needed was a male child
who would live. . . . " Am I not a man like other men ? "
he exclaimed to Chapuys when the Ambassador reminded him
that he might not have another child. " You do not know my
life. Am I not a man like other men ? "

Anne, the garden wife, had so far only given him a daughter,
Elizabeth. And of what use was that to England.

In the past, soon after the birth of that useless daughter,
Anne had pretended, while Henry was under the sway of another
beauty, to be with child once more, in order to regain her hold
over him — in order, too, that she might remain in England as
Regent when the King went to France, and then carry out her
threat against the life of Mary. So it was thought. But it is
possible that with her violent wish to bear another child, she
actually believed her wish was to be granted. However that
may have been, it is certain that on the winter day when Catherine
lay dead and the whole of life seemed to open before the woman
who had supplanted her, there was no fresh pretence : Anne

D

Boleyn was indeed with child again. And the child, she was convinced, would be a son — her saviour and the country's.

But of England she did not think.

At moments her exultation, and with it, her hatred of the dead woman, rose almost to the height of madness. But this mood alternated with fits of desperate weeping, of a deadly paralysing fear. What would be her fate if the child should not, after all, be a son ? But hatred predominated.

The people loved the injured wife, the rightful Queen, and hated her supplanter. The women saw in her their own danger, their own supplanter, the symbol of their husbands' unfaithfulness. The men saw in her " the whore " for whose sake the trade with Flanders had been ruined. When she appeared in public crowds rose in her path, shrieking defiance at her — rose like dust, and were as quickly gone. When, on Easter Day, a few weeks after her secret marriage, the Prior of Austin Friars prayed for her as Queen, the listening crowds " tumultuously rose and left " although the service was still at its height. Her Queenship counted for nothing.

Even at Court she was not safe : in July 1535, the King's Fool, " ung innocent ", Chapuys called him, had, in front of the whole Court, called the usurper-Queen " Une Ribalde " and her child a bastard. The King was in such a fury that the Fool's life was in danger, and he was hidden by Sir Nicholas Carew, the King's Master of the Horse, until the royal rage had abated.

Chapuys, Anne's deadly enemy, had said before the secret marriage took place, " Pray God the Lady will be content with taking the Queen's jewels and her husband, and will not insist on taking her life as well."

The humiliations that Anne had undergone were due to that dead woman's terrible dignity.

Henry had, it is true, forced Catherine to give up her jewels, in order that her ex-maid of honour might wear them when she accompanied her mistress's husband on his journey to a meeting with the French King. But Anne knew that the Queen had said it was against her conscience to give her jewels to adorn a person who was the scandal of Christendom, and a disgrace to the King who flaunted her before such a company.

There was yet something she must take from the Queen whose male children did not live much beyond their birth — the mother of the little child whose short life, from the 1st of January to the 22nd of February 1511, is thus recorded in one of the Manuscript Folios of the Chapter House in Westminster. " In the second year of our lord the King, her Grace the Queen bore a prince, whose soul is now with the holy Innocents of God ". — Three weeks before the birth of Elizabeth, Chapuys reported to the Emperor : ² " The Lady, not being satisfied with what she has already, has solicited the King to ask the Queen for a very rich triumphal cloth which she brought from Spain to wrap up her children with at baptism. The Queen has replied that it has not pleased God that she should . . . grant any favour in a case so horrible and abominable."

Anne Boleyn had not forgotten those answers. She knew, too, that five months before the second answer was given, the Imperial Ambassador had told his master, " a sentence of excommunication is the sovereign and only remedy, and the Queen says the King would not struggle against it, if only for fear of his subjects. . . . If a struggle arose I do not know if the Lady, who is hated by all, would escape with her life and her jewels."

The threat of excommunication grew nearer after the death on the scaffold of Bishop Fisher and Sir Thomas More. Pope Paul III framed a Bull of interdiction and deposition, " which," says Froude, " though reserved at the moment in deference to Francis of France, and not issued till three years later, was composed in the first burst of his displeasure. The substance of his voluminous anathemas may be thus briefly epitomised.

" . . . Already lying under the censures of the Church, he (Henry) had gone on to heap crime on crime ; and therefore, a specific number of days being allowed him to repent and make his submission, at the expiration of this period of respite the following sentence was to take place :

" The King, with all who abetted him in his crimes, was to be pronounced accursed — cut off from the Body of Christ, to perish. When he died, his body should lie without burial ;

his soul blasted with anathema, should be cast into Hell for ever. The lands of his subjects who remained faithful to him were to be laid under an interdict : their children were to be disinherited, their marriages, pronounced illegal, their wills, invalid ; only by one condition could they escape their fate — by instant rebellion against the apostate prince. All officers of the crown were absolved from oaths ; all subjects, secular or ecclesiastic, from their allegiance : the entire nation, under penalty of excommunication, was commanded no longer to acknowledge Henry as their sovereign. No true son of the church should hold intercourse with him or his adherents. They must neither trade with them, speak with them, or give them food. The clergy, leaving behind a few of their members to baptize the new-born infants, were to withdraw from the accursed land, and return no more till it had submitted. If the King, trusting to force, persevered in his iniquity, the lords and commons of England dukes, marquises, earls, and all other persons, were required, under the same penalty of excommunication, to expel him from his throne ; and the Christian princes of Europe were called on to show their fidelity to the Holy See by aiding so godly a work.

"In conclusion, as the King had commanded his clergy to preach against the Pope in their churches, so the Pope commanded them to retaliate upon the King, and with bell, book and candle declare him cursed." [3]

The King remained unafraid. In March 1531, he told Chapuys that if the Pope issued ten thousand excommunications, he would not care a straw for them. When the Papal Nuncio hurled at him the sentence of excommunication and a papal appeal to the secular arm, Henry declared he cared nothing for either. He would open the eyes of Princes, he said, to show them how small was really the power of the Pope. And when the Pope had done what he liked on his side, Henry would do what he liked here. [4]

The King had thus braved the threat of excommunication, caring nothing. But the Lady, to whom the Imperial Ambassador referred, often, as " la grande putain " (" the great whore "), knew the fear that reigned over the King's heart,

and on this she set herself to play, after finding a false prophet
who would be her mouthpiece.

The marriage of the King to the witch-Queen had been
heralded by portents in the heavens. At the end of October
1532, three months before that event, Archbishop Cranmer
informed the King that while he himself had only seen the giant
comet in the east, a blue cross had been observed, by others,
above the moon, together with a flaming horse-head and a
flaming sword. " What strange things these tokens do signify
to come hereafter, God knoweth, for they do not appear but
against some great mutation."

He added that " many of our household are dead of the
plague ".

Henry braved the portents as he had braved the Pope. But
were he threatened with the extinction of his male line, the
portents and prophets would appear to him in a different light.

The sheet-lightnings of the fires of the martyrdoms lit the
whole countryside, and beside them walked processions of
darkened or falsely illuminated beings. Lit by those flares,
and by the garish horror of that unspoken, appalling blasphemy
the Blood of Hales — (bird-lime coloured with ochre, com-
pounded by priests, to which the people flocked in thousands,
believing, in the words of Archbishop Cranmer, " that it is the
very Blood of Christ, and that the sight of it puts all men in a
state of salvation ") — amid the cries of " Antichrist is come,"
" The Millennium is here," " There are no fires in Hell," " The
Host is but Worms' meat," " The Host is but Jack-in-the-Box "
— lit by those flares and accompanied by those wandering cries,
the false saints and prophets born from the time had their being.
That Cassandra of the depths, Elizabeth Barton, " The Nun of
Kent ", the semi-epileptic servant-girl who brought about her
own death and that of many famous men by her prophecies,
was the most remarkable of these ; indeed, as Froude said, " she
held in her hand the balance of the fortunes of England ".

Servant to one Cobb (bailiff to Archbishop Warham at
Aldington in Kent), she was seized, at the age of twenty-six,
with genuine illness, accompanied by attacks of violent hysteria
during which she saw visions and gave forth prophecies. During

one of these attacks the Virgin Mary appeared to her and ordered her to leave the bailiff and devote herself to the exclusive service of the Virgin, by whom she was especially beloved. "Being laid before the image of Our Lady, her face was wonderfully disfigured, her tongue hanging out, and her eyes being in a manner plucked out and laid upon her cheeks, and so greatly deformed. There was then heard a voice speaking within her belly, as it had been in a tonne, her lips not greatly moving . . . the which voice when it told anything of the joys of heaven, spake so sweetly and so fearfully, that every man was ravished with the hearing thereof, and contrariwise, when it told anything of hell, it spoke so horribly and terribly, that it put the hearers at great fear." . . .⁵

Used by a fraudulent priest, Father Bocking, as a ventriloquist's dummy, this singular being was soon regarded as a saint and inspired prophetess throughout the country. Once, she actually made her way into the King's presence, and, to his face, with serpentine writhings and contortions changing suddenly to the stiffness of a ventriloquist's dummy, she prophesied his doom, calling down woe upon his marriage with Anne Boleyn, and warning him that he must die within the year.

The King remained silent, staring at her unwaveringly with those formidable eyes. Then the epileptic who "believed the world when she found the world believed in her" (Froude), turned to the ancient and doddering Archbishop Warham, who had promised to celebrate the King's marriage to Anne Boleyn, and frightened him from his purpose. He, at her request, "brought her to Wolsey, then tottering at the edge of ruin . . . and he, too, in his perplexity, was frightened and doubted".⁶

The Nun of Kent was a partisan of Catherine. But another being of this sort was suborned by the Concubine to declare he had received a revelation from God that it was impossible for Anne to conceive a son while the true Queen and her daughter lived. It was said that the news of this revelation had reached the King. Certainly the Concubine had sent the prophet to be interviewed by Cromwell.

For the lightness of Anne Boleyn masked a terrible will. Like that daughter in whose reign England was to begin her greatness, Anne Boleyn "danced high". But she did not, like that daughter, "dance disposedly". An old and great man,* waiting for death in the Tower, asked his daughter one day how the Queen fared. "Never better," she replied. "There is nothing in the Court but dancing and sporting." "Alas," he sighed, "it pitieth me — to think into what misery she will shortly come. Those dances of hers will spurn off our heads like footballs, but it will not be long ere she will dance headless."

* Sir Thomas More.

NOTES TO CHAPTER FIVE

[1] Paul Friedmann, *Life of Anne Boleyn.*
[2] July 30, 1533.
[3] Froude, *Henry VIII.*
[4] A. F. Pollard, *Henry VIII.*
[5] Letter from Archbishop Cranmer, quoted in Sir Henry Ellis' *Original Letters Illustrative of English History*, vol. iii.
[6] Froude, *Henry VIII.*

Chapter Six

THOSE dancing feet did not spurn off the head of Wolsey, the King's principal Minister, but they helped to kick him to the dust. The great Cardinal, by the King's orders, had forced Henry Percy, afterwards Earl of Northumberland, to relinquish Anne, his love. But he had done worse than this. When Anne had put ambition in the place of love, the Cardinal had, or so she thought, been dilatory in his efforts to bring about the annulment of the King's marriage : had even, perhaps, plotted to stop it. So the Cardinal must go.

This great but evil man, who was yet beloved by all who served him, this " mass of physical corruption lit by the red glow in the eyes " ¹ — this Cardinal " with the bloodie gloves worn lest he should be cold in the midst of these ceremonies ",* had helped to build up the power of England, in order to increase his own personal greatness. He desired, according to Falier, " not so much to be honoured as a prince as to be adored like God. He is grasping, and receives presents like a King." " Nothing pleases him more ", wrote Giustinian in 1519, " than to be called the Arbiter of Christendom."

At this time " the position ² which England held in the Councils of Europe was a marvellous advance upon that which it occupied in 1509. . . . The first ten years of Henry's reign had been a period of fluctuating, but continued progress. Wolsey was able to play off the mutual jealousies (of the Empire and France) so as to reassert England's position. He imposed a general peace, or rather truce, which raised England even higher than the treaties of 1514 had done, and made her appear as the conservator of Europe. England has almost usurped the place of the Pope as mediator between rival Christian princes."

But with these triumphs, Wolsey's pride had grown. During the first months after Giustinian's arrival in England, Wolsey would say " His Majesty will do so-and-so." After a while,

* A contemporary writer.

this was changed to "*We* will do so-and-so." By 1519 he was saying "*I* shall do so-and-so." He behaved to the Emperor as to an equal, and, when they met at Bruges, did not dismount from his mule, but merely doffed his cap and "embraced as a brother the temporal head of Christendom ".[3] He would allow, as a privilege, Ambassadors to kiss his hands. Bishops invested him with his robes, and must kneel to put on his sandals.

Then the power of Wolsey waned.

At the time of the Cardinal's death, "wars had been made [4] from which England derived no visible profit. Not an acre of territory had been acquired, the wealth amassed by Henry VII had been squandered, and Henry VIII in 1529 was reduced to searching for gold mines in England." "England had been raised to the highest place in the Councils of Europe by 1521, but the fall was quite as rapid, and in 1525, she counted for less than she had done in 1513."

Wolsey's power over the King was ascribed, by popular belief, not to the fact that he was a great Minister, but to his knowledge of the Black Arts.

He was held, by contemporaries, to have cast the King's nativity, and to have made, "by craft of necromancy", graven images. He knew much that was in the King's mind, for Henry's confessor, and most of his companions, were the Cardinal's familiars.

Anne Boleyn knew this, and fawned upon the Cardinal. She smiled up at the thick white face with its heavy jowl and fat fleshy nose with thick nostrils. She looked laughingly into the red glow of the eyes that were set in heavy dark rings as if the brain behind them never slept.

He hated her as much as she hated him, yet he gave her rich presents, and she, in a letter of thanks (1528), declared that "all the days of my life I am most bound, of all creatures, next to the King's grace, to love and serve your Grace. I beseech you never to doubt that I shall vary from this thought while truth is in my body." She would send messages to the Cardinal, saying she feared he had forgotten her, as he had sent her no token ; and once, when the King sent down a dish to Anne for her supper, she said she "wished she had some good meat from the Cardinal, such as carps or shrimps ".

Sometimes, even before Anne had gained full power over the King, there were underground contests between her and the great Cardinal. There was the case of the evil nun — Eleanor Carey, sister-in-law to Mary Boleyn. At the time of the sweating sickness, the Abbess of Wilton died, and the choice of her successor lay with the Cardinal. Anne wished Eleanor Carey to become Abbess, although it was proved that she was " of dissolute life, and the mother of several illegitimate children ".[5] Wolsey wished to appoint Dame Isabel Jordan, an " aged, sad and discreet woman ", but the friends of Eleanor Carey raked up an old scandal against this rival claimant. Wolsey, however, appointed his " sad " choice, and Anne, although she caused him to be rebuked by the King, continued to *pretend* friendship towards him, for the moment had not yet come in which she might strike at him with impunity.

But when Anne had gained full ascendancy over the King, and the Cardinal could serve her no longer, he found that there was " a night-crow that possessed the royal ear against him, and misrepresented all his actions " — " the night-crow, the enemy that never slept, but studied night and day, and continually imagined his destruction ". Chapuys told the Emperor " The Duke of Norfolk, the Lady and her father have not ceased to plot against the Cardinal ; especially the Lady, who does not cease to weep and regret her lost youth and her honour, threatening the King that she would leave him, in sort that he had much trouble to appease her ; though the King prayed, most affectionately, even with tears in his eyes, that she would not speak of leaving him ".

He even went so far, in order to show her that he was in earnest about the annulment of his marriage, as to allow her to hide behind a screen while he gave audience to the Emperor's Ambassador, in order that she might overhear all that was said.

But nothing would satisfy her, short of the arrest of the Cardinal.

He was so hated by the Boleyn faction, that the Duke of Norfolk, Anne's uncle, hearing that Wolsey was partially restored to favour and was considering returning to Court, sent him a message that "unless he moved northwards, he would tear him to pieces with his teeth".

The total downfall of Wolsey was brought about by a charge that he had written to Rome asking that he might be reinstated in certain possessions taken from him, at the beginning of his disgrace, by Henry, — and that he had also solicited France to act in his favour. Further, he was accused of having taken such huge bribes from abbots and priests, laid such yearly impositions on "hospitals where many poor people were relieved", "that they were no longer able to keep hospitality as they were used to do, which is a great cause that there be so many beggars, vagabonds, and thieves".

Nor was this all. "Since they have had the Cardinal's physician," wrote Chapuys, "they have found what they sought, for . . . he lived in the Duke of Norfolk's house like a prince. He is singing the tune as they wished him."

The physician was Dr. Agostino, a Venetian, who, "wearing a boisterous gown of black velvet",[6] had, one day at dinner, overthrown with the swirl of that gown a great cross which stood in the corner of the room and which, in its fall, cut the head of Bonner. This gravely disturbed the Cardinal, who declared it to be a bad omen, and withdrew himself from the table to pray.

Now Dr. Agostino was to help overthrow a human life. A new charge was brought against the Cardinal. That imposing figure, with his scarlet gloves that matched his scarlet hat, his nosegay, and his perpetual cry of "The King and I", had brought, it was said, "the King's Majesty into marvellous danger, for knowing himself to have the foul and contagious disease of the great pox, broken out upon him in divers parts of his body, he had come daily to His Grace, blowing upon him with his perilous and infective breath".

This plague, as we have seen in the first chapter of this book, was then sweeping Europe, exceeding the medieval curse of leprosy in its universality, rivalling it in its symptoms. Hidden by Cardinals' robes and by beggars' rags, this disease, "the pyning of the pox", "the Neopolitan scurf", "the Neopolitan Favours", the "French marbles", as it was variously called, destroyed Thomas Wolsey in his Cardinal's Palace, and Puffing Dick, King of the Beggars, in the overhanging horror of the slums. When Lorenzo de Medici, usurper-Duke of Urbino, was married, the Sieur de Floranges wrote that the young bride "did not marry the Duke of Urbino alone, for the pox was also her bridegroom. And this very day the King" (of France) "made him a Knight of his Order." Catherine de Medici was the child of that double marriage. Contracted in his youth, after the battle of Flodden, this plague crept through the veins of King Henry, and, through his tainted blood, destroyed his sons at their birth, or in their adolescence.

Wolsey died in his disgrace — not by the axe, or directly from the pox, but from some sudden and mysterious illness that may have been due to poison, administered by his own hand. Immediately after his death, Lord Wiltshire gave, in celebration, an entertainment at which a play was performed, in the presence of Anne, of her brother, the Duke of Norfolk, and their friends at Court, representing the Cardinal's descent into Hell.

Nothing remained of that power which had been so great. And now Anne, the crowned Queen, urged that her former mistress, and that mistress's daughter, must be put to death — raging at the King, taunting him, saying ever that it was a disgrace to the realm and to him that they were not punished as traitresses.

In December 1533, three months after the birth of Elizabeth, the Duke of Suffolk was ordered to take Queen Catherine by force to a house surrounded by deep water and marshes, "the most unhealthy and pestilential house in England". "The King", wrote Chapuys, "at the solicitations of the Lady, whom he dares not contradict, had determined to place the Queen in this house; and the King and the Lady have agreed to shut up the Queen in this island, and, failing all other pretexts, to accuse her of being insane" — like her sister Queen Juana of Castille, the Emperor's mother, who lived, for forty-nine years, in raging madness.

The Queen locked herself into her apartments, and told

the Commission through the door that if they wished to remove her they must drag her from the house by force.

She was then left undisturbed; and here for a time, in a house nearly as gloomy as that, surrounded by water and marshes, to which she was to have been taken, she lived, rising in the depth of each night to pray, as if she were a nun; rising to dress, each morning, at five o'clock; wearing always, beneath her dress, the rough habit of St. Francis of the First Order, of which she was a member; and, at each hour of the day and night, fearing either death by poison, or to be struck down by assassins hidden in her room, or that she would meet with some other sudden doom, far from the eyes of men.

This fear was like a miasma, or the infection from some strange disease; it spread around her, until everyone connected with her became affected — Chapuys, her servants, her daughter Mary, who had been taken from her, and whom she would never see again. . . .

For in Mary's mind there were now only two thoughts; her mother's danger, real or imagined, and her own chance of escape from England. In answer to secret messages from the Emperor's Ambassador, she said that she thought it would be easy to escape from the house, if she were given something with which to drug her women. She would have to pass the window of the *governante*, Lady Shelton (who was a Boleyn by birth, and the aunt of Anne), but once she was out of the house, she could break open the garden gate without difficulty. There were other dangers, however. Chapuys feared she might be watched, and that the ports might have been warned.

During one of those illnesses which were becoming increasingly frequent with the Princess, Sir William Butts, the King's physician, in conference with the Queen's, said openly that "unless the King fell ill, in which case he might listen to remonstrances, — or unless force were used, the lives of the Queen and the Princess were in danger ".

That peril, Chapuys believed, was imminent, and whatever was done, must be done quickly. The King, hearing that the Princess was ill, had ridden over to the house where she was living, and had ordered Lady Shelton to tell the Princess she was his most dangerous enemy — it was for her sake that the Powers of Christendom were enraged against him. What was this, Chapuys asked himself, but a hint that no punishment would fall on whoever encompassed the Princess's death — if it were done discreetly ?

The escape of Mary was planned for February 1536. A revolt would follow in March or April, Henry would be dethroned, and Mary put in his place. — But another grave illness of Mary's put a stop to the plan, and the Princess remained under the supervision of Lady Shelton, who was then warned by Chapuys that, should the Princess die while in her charge, she would be held responsible — the same warning being repeated by Sir William Butts. The result was that whenever Princess Mary had a headache, the house resounded with Lady Shelton's cries and lamentations. The Ambassador also handed the *governante* small bribes which she, sly, watchful, changeable, and full of fear, yet not, one believes, bad-hearted, accepted, giving in return small privileges and, then in a fright, withdrawing them again.

Meanwhile Anne, or so the Ambassador believed, wove other plots for the undoing of Mary. She had, indeed, changed into the stepmother of a fairy story. She had boasted that she would make the Princess her maid. She had induced the King to deprive his eldest daughter of her state as Princess, and to send her to the household of his youngest daughter, the child of Anne, as a dependant. She had sent a message to Lady Shelton, ordering that if Mary persisted in retaining her state as Princess, and refused to eat at the common table, she was to be deprived of food, beaten and buffeted, and treated as " the cursed bastard that she was ".

The Concubine intended, so the Ambassador thought (and in this and the preceding chapters we see Anne Boleyn through his eyes), to bring about the Princess's death, if not from violence, then from grief. Or if this failed, to bring about her moral fall, her disgrace, in order to force her to renounce her right to the throne, and give excuse for ill-treating her.

But now, with the failure of these plans, this Lamia-like being seemed to change : her darkness was gone. Arriving without warning at Hatfield, to visit her own child, she sent word to the Princess to come and make her obeisance to Anne as Queen. Should she do this, the message ran, she would find in Anne a second mother, who would calm the King's wrath and intercede with him that the Princess should take her right place at Court.

But the Princess replied that she knew of no Queen in England excepting her mother. She would, however, be grateful if Lady Anne Boleyn would intercede with the King on her behalf.

At this rebuff, the stepmother's rage was not to be controlled. It was increased by the fact that she knew the King could not entirely kill his feeling for his eldest daughter ; for Mary was his child, and therefore possessed semi-Divine qualities. In spite of his breach with her mother, in spite of the constant anger roused in him by the Emperor's interference with his private affairs, the King still loved her. In a rage he would threaten her life, and yet there were moments when he remembered her as she had been when she was a little child, before his anger against her mother, his infatuation with Anne, had begun. " By God," he had told the Venetian Ambassador, " this baby never cries." He loved children, and this was, perhaps, the only tenderness and sweetness in his nature. Mary had been the object of his love and his pride when she was a little helpless creature, and still the tenderness clung to his heart. In his eyes she was beautiful, and even his disappointment that she was not a son could not take away his pride in her. He could not restrain himself from speaking of her with love. She was obstinate, he said to the French and Imperial Ambassadors — but that was the fault of her Spanish blood : she took after her mother. Yet what virtues — what gifts ! And tears showed in the King's puffed eyes. He made excuses for her, and that enraged her stepmother still more.

Now when the new Queen Anne complained to Henry, his answers were evasive. He looked at her strangely. Something was happening in the King's mind — a change that she did not understand.

She had never understood anything in his nature, excepting the elementary fact that if something he wanted was withheld from him, his desire for it grew. She did not understand his gigantic vanity, nor his sense of kingship, and so she had raged at him, tried to rule him. She did not understand his occasional simplicities, and thought she could rule the man who would become a country squire for a few hours, thanking Jaspar, the old gardener at Beaulieu, for bringing the first strawberries, cherries, and cucumbers, or talking to Hannibal Zinzaro and Alexander the Rider about medicine for the royal horses.

Above all, she did not understand that with all the deformities, the monstrous pride of his nature, he was yet a great King.

" In spite of his appalling obstinacy to the end of his days," wrote Professor Pollard,[7] " he valued a counsellor who would honestly maintain what the King desired. Those counsellors to whom he gave his confidence were never minions or servile flatterers. Henry had his Court favourites with whom he hunted and shot and diced, played tennis, primero, the game of Pope July . . . but they never influenced his policy. Ministers might flatter themselves that they would rule his mind and calculate his actions, but it is quite certain that no minister read so clearly his master's mind as the master read his minister's." . . . " Three people may keep counsel," said the King in 1530,[8] " if two be away ; and if I thought that my cap knew my counsel, I would cast it in the fire and burn it."

This was the man whom first Wolsey, then Anne Boleyn, had tried to rule.

Listening to his new Queen, as, in her rages, she revealed her vanities, her self-seeking greed, the King began to notice things to which he had blinded himself. He still watched her every movement — but not from love : he was seeing for the first time her empty pretensions, her unfitness to be Queen.

Now, tired of her fascinations, wearied by those pretensions, he began to blame her for all his misfortunes.

He remembered certain incidents : she had shown complete heartlessness when Catherine, the Princess-Dowager, his sister-in-law and the mother of Mary, had died. She had even worn yellow at that time (so had he, but of that he did not think). . . . Many great men had died because of her. Sir Thomas More had been one of these, and Anne had cared nothing.

When the news of More's execution came, the King was playing a game of cards with his new Queen. He rose to his feet and looked at her : to see her, you would have thought that nothing untoward had happened. " Thou art responsible for this man's death," he told her, and so saying, left the room.

What had he got from the marriage for which he had risked so much ? Gusts of rage, an endless emptiness, — and a useless daughter.

Even as long ago as the spring of 1531, she had given way to violent attacks of rage, due to delay in the annulment of Henry's marriage with Catherine ; attacking the King, she had used language so violent that he complained to the Duke of Norfolk : Queen Catherine, he said, had never in his life " used ill words towards him ". Now, as Queen, Anne felt no need for restraint, either in speech or manner.

The King was bored. To this, after all these years of infatuation, she had brought him. And the boredom increased, day by day.

Anne Boleyn knew that, almost from the moment of their marriage, he had been unfaithful to her — in mind, at any rate : and there had been days when a cold fear invaded her heart. But the King would grow tired of the new love, the fear passed, and Anne continued in her old arrogant way. The violence of her pride was such that she constantly told the King he was more bounden to her than man had ever been to woman. Had she not saved him from a state of deadly sin ? Was it not through her that he was now the richest prince in Christendom, since, for her sake, he had confiscated the Church properties ? Was not the reformation of the Church in England brought about for love of her ? What did not the King and the nation owe her ?

So she continued in her summer pride. But those eyes which she had thought were closed for ever, did not cease to follow her, although Anne, on her side, must have relaxed her vigilance.

" She waxing great again," said George Wyatt, in his Memoir of Queen Anne Boleyn, " and not so fit for dalliance, the time was taken to steal the King's affection from her, when most of all she was to have been cherished. And he once showing to bend from her, many that least ought, shrank from her, and some

E

leant to the other side ; such are the flexible natures of those in Courts, of princes for the most part."

At first the new Queen had not noticed, with any particular interest — although she had seen and watched the other light and fleeting loves of the King — a slim young woman whose face had a strange and rather beautiful greenish pallor, like that of the flower of the hellebore. Anne, in the time of her ascendancy, held the King by her summer boldness and loud laughter. This woman was silent and slinking, and when she spoke, it was of virtue and duty. Above all, she was meek. For she had been well taught by the enemies who had watched Anne, and she was an apt pupil. It was some time before the Queen noticed that the King had singled out this young woman for attention. Then " there was often scratching and bye-blows between the Queen and her maid ", whose name was Jane Seymour.[9]

Now, on her way into the depths, on this January day, the usurper-Queen, opening the door before which we saw her pause, found, in the small room beyond, this insignificant maid of honour. She was sitting upon the King's knee.*

On the very day of the funeral of the Queen whom Anne had supplanted, all hopes of an heir to the throne ceased. After some hours of a slow-dragging agony, the new Queen gave premature birth to a dead child.

And that child was a son.

Entering her room, merciless, without pity for her pain or her humiliation, the King, fixing her with his formidable stare, told her that he knew, now, that God would not grant him male children. — " I will speak to you," he said, " when you are well."

Then, according to Wyatt, " some words were heard to break out of the inward feeling of her heart's dolour, laying the fault upon his unkindness, which the King, more than was cause . . . took more hardly than otherwise if he had not been somewhat too much overcome with grief, or so much alienate ".

Weeping, she said she was not like the dead Queen — she could not bear to see him in the arms of another. Yes, it was what he had done, together with her fear when the Duke of

---

* This is a well-known story, but no one can vouch for the accuracy. Certainly something must have happened, to account for Anne's sudden illness.

Norfolk told her the King had fallen from his horse — (for even at this moment she could not forget her hatred of her uncle, her wish to injure him) — that had killed the child.

Then from the primitive bulk, the Minotaur who was King, tears fell.

But it was for himself, and for his country, that he wept.

Rising, he left the room, and soon afterwards the Palace of Greenwich.

For the rest of the time that remained to her, Anne Boleyn was alone with her splendour.

NOTES TO CHAPTER SIX

[1] Garrett Mattingley, *Katherine of Aragon.*
[2] A. F. Pollard, *Henry VIII.*
[3] *Venetian Calendar,* iii. 298.
[4] A. F. Pollard, *Henry VIII.*
[5] Paul Friedmann, *Life of Anne Boleyn.*
[6] Cavendish, *Life of Wolsey.*
[7] A. F. Pollard, *Henry VIII.*
[8] Cavendish, *Life of Wolsey.*
[9] *Life of Jane Dormer, afterwards Duchess of Feria.*

Chapter Seven

THE hand of that dead child signed the death-warrant of Anne Boleyn. But the spring months were to ripen almost to summer before her ghost would leave the Palace. Now when her father, loud and meaningless as the wind, and her brave and reckless brother were in her company, they seemed like dear ghosts from a well-remembered past. Only it was she who was dead, and her brother was walking down the long galleries of the Palace to meet her and share her death. That other ghost, these younger dead would leave behind them, to drag out his dishonoured days in the shadow of the Palace.

She had no longer any interest in life, excepting at those moments when a feverish longing for excitement would invade her blood, make her speak rashly, like a person in delirium. What interest could remain in that high and empty life ?

Her child Elizabeth was far away, at the nursery-palace at Hunsdon, and in any case what could she mean to her mother ? It was the birth of that useless daughter that had begun her downfall.

But the days must be passed, somehow, until the moment when her own nature, and fear and hope, tyranny and pride, would be at peace.

Those days were spent in an aimless wandering in the gardens of the Palace at Greenwich, by the waterside. Or she would sit, for hours, in a courtyard, playing with the great wolf-hound, Urien, who was now very old. Sometimes she thought of " little Purkoy ", the dog whom she had loved best, and who had died from a fall, and nobody had dared tell her, until the King himself had done so.

And as she thought of little Purkoy, she would awake as from a deep sleep, and find tears upon her cheek. Oh, why should one weep because something one loves is dead, and has nothing more to fear ?

As we see her now, in her loneliness, can she truly be the

woman whom Chapuys thought he had seen, plotting cruelties against the helpless Mary ? Or had unhappiness wrought this change in her ?

The usurper-Queen knew that her youth and her beauty were fading like the young petals blown by the spring wind, and would soon be gone.

So she drifted through her days, alone. The King spoke to her but rarely. And he had told one about the Court that he was seduced into this marriage by witchcraft, and so regarded it as null. " It was evident, since God did not permit them to have a male issue."

Her enemies knew this, and the way was even now being prepared for her death, a pretext was being found.

Even before the death of Catherine, there had been moments when the usurper-Queen felt some presage of her fate. One day at a Court festival at Greenwich, finding herself alone for a moment with Palamedes Gontier, secretary to Philippe de Chabot, Admiral of France, then on an embassy to England for the purpose of negotiating a marriage between the baby Elizabeth and the baby Duc d'Angoulême — she asked him hurriedly, and in a low voice, why he had stayed so long in France. It had engendered strange thoughts and suspicions, and doubts in the mind of the King : " Doutes, étranges pensemens — doutes et soupçons ".[1] She implored him to tell the Admiral he must so act towards the King that she would not be utterly lost, for she saw herself very near that, and in more danger than before her marriage. She could not speak as fully as she wished . . . She was afraid to speak — yes, afraid. There were eyes watching her, those of the King and of the lords at Court. . . . She stopped and looked round, adding in a still lower voice, " I cannot stay longer nor see you again, nor write ".[2] She then left him. And the King, who had stood watching her for a moment, went into the ballroom, she accompanying him.

The new Queen felt those eyes upon her, and lived her high laughing fateful life, half in fear, half in pride.

She could not walk down a gallery of the Palace but unseen watchers peered at her through the half-open doors of rooms she believed to be empty. Not a word spoken by her but echoed through those vast seemingly uninhabited rooms until it reached the ears of those who were plotting her destruction. But she said to herself that all her enemies had been overcome, one by one. Had she not even destroyed the growing power of that shadowy masked beauty whose ascendancy over the King had once threatened her — but whose name, so utterly was she overthrown, has not even come down to us ? We see only some glimpse of that laughing lovely face, and then it is gone, as if bright great leaves had cast a network of shadow across it, darkening it and hiding it from our view.

And thinking of the overcome beauty, of Catherine, of Wolsey, the heart of Anne fluttered like a bird : she became increasingly unwise in talk and action.

She had always been indiscreet in her speech, as when, before it was known that she was married to the King, she had told Wyatt and a group of other courtiers that she had a longing for apples, and that when she said this to the King he had replied that she must be with child. But that, she had assured him, was not so. And looking round at their astonished faces, she screamed with laughter, to their great embarrassment.

She had always laughed too loudly and too long, and at moments when no laughter should have been heard. Simonette, her French governess, scolded her every day of her childhood for this habit of shrieking with laughter that had almost the sound of terror.

One winter day before her marriage, coming into a Palace room, lit only by the white light of the cinnamon-sweet snow, she had laughed at a book of prophecies placed by some unknown hand on the window-sill — a book of the same kind as the prophetic hieroglyphic almanacs of later centuries. Picking it up, and turning over the pages idly, Anne Boleyn called to her principal maid of honour, Anne Saville — for although she was not yet married, she was given the state of a Queen, or of the wife of a great noble :

" Come hither, Nan," said she, " see here this book of prophecies " (pointing to three figures marked H. K. and A.). " This is the King, this is the Queen, and this is myself, with my head cut off."

Anne Saville answered, "If I thought it true, I would not myself have him, were he an emperor."

"Tut, Nan," said her mistress, "I think the book a bauble, and am resolved to have him, that my issue may be royal, whatever may become of me."

And her laughter rang through the Palace room.

Soon, a few light and laughing words, spoken in passing to a Court musician, and unwary speeches to two of her husband's gentlemen-in-waiting, were to bring about her death.

Those great slanting black eyes were not gifted with near sight. Their gaze was fixed on something far away, on the mountain heights. She only half discerned the features of those who stood next to her. She had never, for instance, scanned the face of Thomas Cromwell, first Chief Secretary, then Lord Privy Seal, so as to understand what was masked by their joviality. That apparently good-humoured, even witty face, of a rather porcine cast, with thick lips, double chin, and a long fleshy nose, whose character was altered slightly by the heavy eyebrows lifting upwards at the temples, and the eyes which had a sudden, sideways, witty glance — that face, ugly yet full of a curious charm, seeming always as if it were about to break into a laugh, could change into the face of Moloch.

This extraordinary man, the son of a blacksmith at Putney, had passed some time in the counting-house of a merchant in Venice, and had been present at the Sack of Rome. According to Cardinal Pole, Cromwell openly avowed to him his Machiavellian principles. He had learned, he said, "that vice and virtue were but names, fit indeed to amuse the leisure of the learned in their colleges, but pernicious to the man who seeks to rise in the courts of Princes. The great art of the politician was, in his judgment, to penetrate through the disguise which sovereigns are accustomed to throw over their real inclinations, and to devise the most specious expedients by which they may gratify their appetites, without appearing to outrage morality or religion."

Yet, according to Cavendish's Life of Wolsey, "by reason of his honest behaviour in his master's" (Wolsey's) "cause, he grew into such estimation in every man's opinion, that he was esteemed to be the most faithfullest servant of his master of all others ".

He was not without heart, and Mary, who had known him since her early childhood, was strongly attached to him.

Yet after the death of Anne, Lord Privy Seal Cromwell told Chapuys that it was he who had begun to form (" fantasier et conspirer ") the situation which brought about the death of the new Queen and her brother, because they were bringing disaster on Europe, preventing a friendship with the Emperor, and interfering in all public affairs.

Actually, Cromwell must now choose between sacrificing his own life and those of the Boleyn brother and sister, for his position was desperate.

Once among their chief supporters (since he and they were in accord on the subject of depriving the Church of its last shreds of independence), there was now a breach between them — brought about partly by the fact that Cromwell wished that Mary should be admitted to be legitimate, as born in *bona fide parentum*. — This he wished, because it would deprive the malcontents of an excuse for rebellion, and because it would ameliorate the quarrel with the Emperor. To this Anne would not agree, and she and her brother now hated him. Lord Wiltshire, with his weakness and rapacity, could be managed. But there was no hope of reconciliation with his children : they were unforgiving, long-memoried, ferocious in hatred as they were loving in friendship.

They must go. But Cromwell knew that he must act cautiously.

He was not without supporters : their uncle, the Duke of Norfolk, had been insulted constantly by Anne, and in such terms that those who heard them blushed, and the Duke was constrained to leave her presence. In addition, both he and Bishop Gardiner believed that she was the only obstacle to the King's return to the See of Rome, and reconciliation with the Emperor.

Most important of all, Chapuys, consulted about the downfall of Anne, had obtained the sanction of Princess Mary — but only to the divorce of the King from " the Concubine ". It is obvious from the Ambassador's letter to the Emperor, written the day after the arrest of Anne, that the Princess had no idea what the charges brought against her mother's supplanter would be, or that they would lead to her death. " She bade me ", wrote Chapuys, " go on with what was to be done ; the more so as it would be for her father's credit and conscience. She had ceased to care whether her father had lawful heirs or not, though such might take away her Crown." — (This because the Emperor had foreseen that danger, should the King set aside " the Concubine ".) " For the sake of God she pardoned every one what had been done against her mother and herself. Acting under her orders, I joined with Cromwell and many other persons. . . ."

The chief agent used by the conspirators was the appalling Lady Rochford, wife to Anne's brother. . . . " He " (Rochford) " was an undesigning generous nobleman ", we are told, but " she abandoned herself to every vice she could gratify in herself or prompt in others ".

This frightful woman now saw the chance to rid herself of the inconvenient presence of her husband. . . . Throughout the whole of this history — and we shall meet her again — we never once see her face . . . catching only the gleam of a dress at the end of a corridor as she, who had been listening at some door vanishes at the sound of approaching footsteps, round the corner of another passage — seeing only a tall shadow waiting outside a closed door for the evil which she had encompassed, to be done in the room beyond.

Here was one instrument. But the plot in which she was to be used must be arranged with care. Cromwell understood the King's disposition, to a certain degree : though he was tired of the Queen, his pride, his certainty that he was invariably in the right, must be considered. " God ", he had assured the Emperor, " has not only made us King by inheritance, but has given us wisdom, policy, and other graces in a most plentiful sort " — adding that " all our laws were founded upon the laws of God, Nature, and honesty, approved by Parliament. . . . I, alone, have acted with the purest faith, and therefore God favours my designs." (This was after the King had left his first wife, and believed that, having departed from his sin, the curse of Heaven would be removed.)

It was necessary to consult the King's conscience, which, though it never prevented the ultimate consummation of his Majesty's wishes, was apt to make the lives of his advisers difficult. That conscience was particularly active on the subject of his own and other people's marriages. Had he not written to Luther, inveighing against the friars who were " wallowing in lust ", with that reformer, as companion and fellow-sinner,—storming at him for marrying, and insisting that he should put aside his wife ?

The King had lectured his errant sister Margaret, Queen Dowager of Scotland, with severity, on the subject of her sinful life. Indeed, one of the causes of his anger against the Pope, at the time he was demanding an annulment of his own marriage, was because this was denied to him, although an annulment was granted to Margaret, on the score of the precontract of her second husband Angus, and because the Queen of Scotland pretended to believe that her late husband, James IV, had not been killed at Flodden Field, but was alive at the time of the marriage.

Actually, the fate of the King of Scots was far stranger. . . . " After the battell," wrote Stow,[3] " the body of the said King was closed in lead and conveyed from thence to London, and to the Monastery of Sheyne in Surrey, where it remained for a time . . . but since the dissolution of that house, in the raigne of Eduard the Sixt, Henry Grey Duke of Suffolk being lodged and keeping house there, I have been shewed the same body lapped in lead close to the head and body, throwne into a waste room amongst the olde timber, leade, and other rubble. Since the whiche time workemen have for their foolish pleasure taken off his head : and Lancelot Young Maister Glaisier to his Majestie, feeling a sweet savour to come from thence, and seeing the same dryed of all moisture, and yet the forme remayning, with the haire of the heade and the bearde redde, brought it to London to his house in Wood Street, where for a time he kept it for the sweetnesse." . . .

King Henry could not be aware that this new form of pot-pourri was in preparation, but he did know that his brother-in-law the King of Scots was dead, and that the widow's excuse for demanding an annulment of her marriage was of a most flimsy nature. He knew, also, that she was living in open adultery with Henry Stuart. He reminded her, therefore, of " the divine ordinance of inseparable matrimony, first instituted in Paradise " and insisted that she should avoid the " inevitable damnation against Advowtrers ".

For he had never, he told himself, been guilty of adultery with Elizabeth Blount, the mother of his son the Duke of Richmond, because he had never, in truth, been married to Catherine.

It seemed wiser, remembering these facts, to persuade the King that anything he wished to do was, necessarily, the thing which God had ordained. Among those pre-ordained happenings was a new marriage. A second divorce was, at this time, impossible. For one thing, Anne would remain Marchioness of Pembroke, with a great income. She and her brother would be the cause of endless trouble in the realm. It was obvious, therefore, that only the guilt of the Queen, and her punishment by death, would free the King from her.

Cromwell considered the character of Squire Harry, and his conscience. Then he began to act.

Hints, veiled at first, were thrown out about the Queen's conduct with other men. Her husband, indifferent to her, bored by her temper and her bold manners, and attracted by another woman, was amused by the stories, which were, as yet, discreet. Then, after a while, he began to understand that his supremacy, as man and as King, were in question. Slowly his anger grew. . . . He even persuaded himself that he felt jealousy.

He remembered those long years before his marriage, when he had longed for her and she had resisted him, because of her " honour ". He thought of his wounded pride, of the day in 1527 when he had written to her saying, " I am in great agony about the contents of your letters, not knowing whether to construe them to my disadvantage, or to my advantage. . . . Having been for more than a year wounded by the dart of love, I am not sure yet whether I shall fail or find a place in your affection." He thought, too, of that other letter which ended " I thank you heartily that you are pleased still to have some remembrance of me ".

She had resisted the King of England, and now she had given herself to a common groom of the chamber (a man of the people) and to various of the King's courtiers.

For the companions of her guilt, real or supposed, were those men who had been most in the company of the King, and so his humiliation became more of a reality in his mind — a physical presence, almost, following him wherever he went.

NOTES TO CHAPTER SEVEN

[1] *Le Laboureur*, i. 405.
[2] Palamedes Goutier to Admiral Chabot, February 5, 1535, *Castelnau Memoirs*.
[3] Stow, *Survey of London*.

Chapter Eight

THE first choice of the astute Cromwell fell upon Mark Smeaton, a man of low birth and colossal vanity, an ex-singing-boy in Wolsey's chapel, and now promoted, because of his skill with the virginals and lute, to be a groom of the chamber. This man was constantly in the King's presence, and was entirely dependent on his bounty; therefore by this choice might the pride of the King be most humiliated. Cromwell chose, also, Francis Weston, one of the most familiar companions of the King and Anne. A year before the marriage of Anne, there is a record in the Privy Purse Expenses, of 16 crowns, paid to her and to young Weston, as their winnings in Pope Julius's game — or Pope July's game, as it was called at Court.*

Henry Norreys was another man to be chosen, and he was the only courtier privileged to follow Henry into his bed-chamber. . . . Thus, by the choice of those familiar companions, who would ever be before the mind's eye of the King, the death of Anne was made certain.

The above was written on the assumption that Anne Boleyn was innocent, and the victim of a plot. That there *was* a plot is certain : but it is possible, of course, that she was guilty, and fell into a trap. It is hardly believable that so many men as those who condemned her, could have been willing to condemn to death a woman whom they knew to be innocent. But again, they may have been suffering from mass hysteria of the kind that arises during a war, when everything is believed. — We shall never know the truth, and can only speculate in the matter.

While the plot was maturing, the King's infatuation for

* This was " a round game ", says Miss Strickland, invented in mockery of Pope Julius II, whose breve of dispensation had been lately produced by Katherine of Aragon, as an important document in favour of the legality of her marriage with Henry VIII : the points were matrimony, intrigue, pope, and the stops ".

Jane Seymour, the strange silent creature with the greenish pallor, the meek contrast to his overbearing wife, the ex-maid of honour to Catherine and the devoted friend of Mary, increased. And there were persons about the Court who, knowing Henry well, advised her how to increase that infatuation still further. . . . Sir Nicholas Carew, Sir Thomas Eliot, and other intimate servants of the King, warned her not to yield to him unless he married her.

One day, when he was absent, the King sent Jane a purse of gold with a letter. She was walking under the green-budding apple trees when she received the messenger. Casting her eyes heavenward, clasping her hands, the virtuous girl fell upon her knees and, kissing the letter, returned it and the gold to the messenger, declaring that her honour was her fortune. If the King wished to give her gold, she added, let him do so when she found a good and worthy husband.

Enchanted by this proof of virtue, Squire Harry (who, in some ways, had a singularly simple mind) swore that such virtue must be respected. In future, he would see Jane Seymour only in the presence of her relatives. So Cromwell (whose son was about to marry Jane's widowed sister, Lady Ughtred) was ordered to vacate a room he occupied in the Palace, so that Jane's brother and his wife might lodge there. And in this room, which could be reached by a secret gallery, Jane received the King and his conscience.

But for all the secrecy, the Court watched and whispered. Soon, a possible new marriage for the King was discussed openly by ambassadors and members of the Court.

On the 24th of April 1536, the preparation for the Queen's attainder began. The King — probably without knowing the reason — gave at Cromwell's request, power to a Commission to "make enquiries as to every kind of treason, by whomsoever committed, and to hold a special commission to try the offenders". The Commission included — one supposes as a blind to its real purpose — the father of Anne.

But the actual charge that was to encompass her death was still to be formulated.

Then one day, the hunted creature, walking through her

presence chamber into her own apartments, saw Mark Smeaton standing looking out of the window. She spoke a few light words with him, and then passed on. . . . She had thought herself alone, excepting for this man. But there must have been some secret, silent listener.

For some time now she had become increasingly indiscreet. . . . Life was so dull, so empty . . . oh for a little pleasure, a little excitement. . . . She hardly cared whence it came.

Idle and bored, it struck her, one April day, that it would be amusing to rally her friend Sir Francis Weston for neglecting his wife, and paying court to Margaret Shelton, daughter of Princess Mary's *governante*, a young woman whom the King had once admired, but who it was now thought would marry Henry Norreys.

The Queen spoke those idle words, and Weston, knowing her vanity, answered equally lightly. . . . Both he and Norreys, he told the Queen, were really in love with — whom did she think? Why, their royal mistress and none other.

Here, at last, was the excitement for which she craved. . . . It would be at least some change in the dullness of her days, if Norreys should answer the same thing. . . . She spoke to him, asking him why he did not marry her cousin Meg. Then, irritated, perhaps, at not receiving the answer for which she had half hoped, she told him he was waiting — she knew it — for dead men's shoes. . . . She said even more.

But Norreys, unlike Weston, looked at her with terror . . . he stared at her as if he was looking Death, not the Queen of England, the familiar Anne, in the face.

She spoke the words that were to condemn them to death, and then passed by, with those dancing feet. . . .

The foolish talk, lightly spoken, was blown away by the spring wind — from one person to another — until the words reached the ears of Cromwell.

It was for this that he had waited. Perhaps he truly believed her guilty, and had plotted only to catch her. In any case, he told Bishop Gardiner, and Wallop, the Ambassador to France, at the time of the trial, that "the Queen's living and other offences towards the King's highness, was so rank and common that her ladies of the privy chamber, and her chamberers " (maids) " could not restrain it within their breasts, but, detesting the same, had so often consultations and conferences of it, that at last it came so plainly to the ears of some of his Grace's counsel, that they could not conceal it from him, but with great fear, as the case enforced, declared what they had heard unto his highness ".

Nor was this all, for those words about a dead man's shoes had been remembered. " There brake out a certain conspiracy of the King's death ", Cromwell told Gardiner, " which extended so far that all we who had the examination of it, quaked at the danger his Grace was in. . . . I write no particulars, the thing be so abominable ; but the like was never heard of."

There were, however, compensations. Cromwell added that Gardiner would receive £100 of the £300 that were " out among these men " (those accused with the Queen), " the third £100 is bestowed of " (on) " the Vicar of Hell " — Sir Francis Bryane, cousin of the woman who was to die, and son of Lady Bryane, the " lady mistress " of little Elizabeth.

The Queen's words with Smeaton were overheard on the last day of April. Next day, this man received an invitation to dine with Cromwell at his house in Stepney — a house surrounded by large gardens, so that nothing that happened within could be heard by those passing by. He went, with no suspicion of danger. A few moments after his arrival there, Cromwell said to him, pleasantly, " Mark, you have spent a great deal of money lately. Whence did that money come ? "

And, as he spoke, this jovial giggling companion changed suddenly to the bullying, brutal power that the monks of the Charterhouse had seen before their martyrdom. Smeaton was seized by his host's servants, and put to the torture of the knotted cord, tightened by means of a stick round the temples. Soon that changed being held in his hands the " confession " of this whimpering broken creature. The " confession " stated that the Queen had given him money, and that she had committed adultery with him three times.

Smeaton was imprisoned in Cromwell's house until the following day.

Meanwhile, the usual May Day tournament was held at Greenwich. The King, with the Queen sitting beside him, seemed in an especially good humour, roaring with laughter, as he spoke to the Ambassadors and to his gentlemen, and calling out remarks to the challengers.

Then something happened. This story was told by the Jesuit Sanders, and repeated by various writers, — that the Queen, either by accident or on purpose, dropped her handkerchief from the gallery while Henry Norreys was passing beneath, and that he picked it up, presumptuously wiped his face with it, then handed it back to the Queen on the point of a lance.

That story the present writer believes to be untrue: no mention is made of it by Cromwell, and the Queen, it is obvious from her demeanour, had no idea what had happened.

In any case, the King suddenly changed colour, and without warning, rose to his feet, left the tilting-yard, and, with a small company of gentlemen, rode towards London.

The Queen returned to her apartments in Greenwich Palace.

She knew that something irrevocable had taken place, but nothing, not even terror, could tell her exactly what had happened. And terror had not yet reached its height. All she felt was a complete deadness, as if all sensibility, all emotion, had been frozen: she existed in a clime where there was neither day nor night.

The beings whom she had thought she knew, treated her still with the respect due to a Queen; yet each person who came into her presence seemed about to break into some message that she had long waited to hear, and that would mean her overthrow.

But that message was not, as yet, ready.

At ten o'clock that night, the first words were delivered to her; although the full meaning, even now, was not clear. Mark Smeaton had been arrested and was imprisoned in the Tower.

Then came the last words of the message. Henry Norreys, also, had been taken to the Tower.

Still the speakers' voices and demeanour showed her an absolute respect. But her heart was invaded by an agony of terror. All around her was an aching horror and void, in which she was utterly alone. She had not even the peace of despair,

F

for at first she thought of flight. Then she knew that she was trapped and doomed, that there was no country, nor person, that would harbour her. The Emperor was her deadly enemy. The French King was bound by a treaty to deliver up English traitors. . . .

In England there was no one to help her ; for her pride and violence had alienated all around her, — even Henry Percy, of whose love she had been certain. Her family was left, but her cowardly, blustering, vacillating father, with whom she had quarrelled, too, when she was *enceinte*, cared for nothing but money, and her brother shared her danger.

Sometimes a terrible lucid calm would sweep over her, and she would ask herself what she had done to bring about that change in those who had loved her.

In her husband, for instance. During their long courtship, when he was the husband of Catherine, he had written to her : " My Mistress and my friend, my heart and I surrender ourselves into your hands, beseeching you to hold us commended to your favour, and that by absence your affection to us may not be lessened : for it would be a great pity to increase our pain, of which absence produces enough and more than I could ever have thought would be felt, reminding us of a point in astronomy, which is this : the longer the days are, the more distant is the sun, and nevertheless the hotter ; so it is with our love, for by absence we are kept a distance from one another, and yet it retains its fervour, at least on my side, I hope the like on yours, assuring you that on my part the pain of absence is already too great for me ; and when I think of the increase of that which I am forced to suffer, it would be almost intolerable, but for the firm hope I have of your unchangeable affection for me."

The letters of Squire Harry to Anne, in that handwriting whose letters seemed branching into small spring leaves, might have been written by a young countryman courting his first love. One bore, for signature, a heart, with, on either side, letters signifying " Henry seeks Anne Boleyn, no other ". . . . And then the word " Rex ". Another bore the signature " H. R." and a heart enclosing the letters A. B. And one had only the King's initials, with the words " Ma aimable " written on either side of the heart.

In those days, he had borne with her endless indiscretions and unwise confidences to those about her. He had even, at that time, endured those bursts of ill-temper which she did not attempt to disguise from him.

What had changed him towards her ?

She had attempted to rule him. And she had borne him, first a daughter, then a dead son.

Next morning she was summoned before the Council and told that she was accused of adultery with three persons, Weston, Norreys, and one unnamed. She might have been already dead and voiceless. " I was cruelly handled at Greenwich," she said in her delirious wandering, when she was in prison. " The Duke of Norfolk would not listen to me. As for Master Treasurer " (her own father) " he was in the Forest of Windsor " — (meaning far away in his mind). " Master Controller was a gentleman. But to be a Queen and so cruelly handled was never seen."

The interrogation ended, the Queen was conducted back to her apartments, and kept under arrest until the tide turned and she could be taken to the Tower.

Then " the Concubine, by the Judgment of God * was brought in full daylight to the Tower " — watched by thousands of eyes, as she had been on the day when she left the Tower to be crowned Queen of England. . . . River-banks, barges, were crowded with spectators come to stare at her downfall.

That night, when the Duke of Richmond, the King's natural son, went to say good-night to his father, the King burst into tears, and embracing him, declared that he and his sister Mary had been watched over by God ; for that cursed and venomous whore had certainly plotted to poison them.

We must now follow that forlorn ghost who was Queen of England, through her wanderings as they were reported to Cromwell by the Constable of the Tower, Sir William Kingston.

She arrived at the Tower at five o'clock, after three hours of a passage in an open barge, exposed to the full view of the

* Chapuys to the Emperor.

staring, semi-exultant crowds. At the Tower there was not a friendly face, not a soul in whose kindness or whose truthfulness she could trust. When she had passed through the Traitors' Gate, "Master Kingston," she asked, trembling, "shall I go to a dungeon?" "No, Madam, you shall go to the lodging you lay in at your Coronatyon." "It is too good for me. Jesu have mercy on me," she whispered, and "knelt down weeping a great space; and in the same period fell into a great laughing". Then, calming herself, she asked that the Eucharist might be exposed next to her chamber, that she might pray for pardon.

Her thoughts were for her brother and her father: she asked continually "O where are they — O where is my sweet brother?" But the Constable, at first, replied evasively.

Did she give one thought to Elizabeth, and to what would be her fate — bastardy, disinheritance, a bleak and hopeless future? We have no record that the name of her child ever crossed her lips, although a few days before her downfall she had sent for her chaplain, and had given him instructions about the child's religious upbringing — almost as if she knew that she, herself, was about to die.

Far away, at the nursery-palace of Hunsdon, England's Prometheus lay sleeping, a little child less than three years old, and over her heart of fire fell the first shadow of the eagle's wing. . . .

On the first night the Queen spent in the Tower, she asked the Constable, "Mr. Kingston, do you know why I am here?" And he said "Nay". "I hear say", said she, "that I shall be accused by three men, and I can say no more than 'nay' unless you shall open my body" — (open it, and expose the heart, as the blackened heart of Katherine had been exposed). "And therewith" (this is the Constable's account) "she opened her gown, adding, 'O Norreys, hast thou accused me? Thou art in the Tower with me: and thou and I shall die together. And Mark, thou art here too.' And then with much compassion she said, 'O my mother, thou wilt die with sorrow.' And then she much lamented my lady Worcester" (being with child) "because her child did not stir in her body." And when the Constable's wife, being present, asked what might be the cause, she said, " It was for the sorrow she took for me ".

Then she said, " Master Kingston, shall I die without justice ? "
To which he replied, " The poorest subject the King hath, had
justice." But at that, she screamed with laughter.

Often she wandered in her speech, and it was those poor,
half-delirious broken sentences which gave those who were
encompassing her death the means wherewith to kill her.

" It is assumed ", wrote her biographer, Mr. Philip W.
Sergeant, " that Brereton, Wyatt and Page were seized through
something she said in her delirium." . . .

For other men had gone to join those already accused —
Smeaton, Weston, and Norreys.

She was never alone. That night, and all the nights that were
to follow until she was led to her death, her aunt Lady Boleyn
(who hated her, and whom she hated), and a certain Mistress
Cosyn, lay on the Queen's pallet, and the Constable and his
wife " at the door without ". " I have everything ", the Constable declared to Cromwell, " told me by Mistress Cosyn."

Chapter Nine

" THE rest of that wretched and forlerne household where "
(she) " lay, knowing what happiness they were to lose
in the world, by want of their liberty, gladly suffered
themselves . . . to be cast into deep and Lethean slumbers, and
so to take away all sense of the paine, yet " (she) " having " (her)
" heart, like Coral which is under water, Continually soft by the
teares that inwardly dropt upon it, was more tender." [1]

Then the tears lay wet upon a cheek and lips that no longer
felt them, and the prisoner slept.

Awakening early from a deep sleep that had been like that
which divides this mortal life from the life everlasting, Anne
Boleyn, for a moment, could not remember where she was.
What were those strange women doing, lying upon her pallet ?

Then terror took the place of the dream-like calm which
she had shown the previous night. Presently, words broke from
the Queen's lips. " This morning ", the Constable told Cromwell,
" she did talk with Mistress Cosyn. And she said that Mr.
Norreys did say on Sunday last unto the Queen's Almoner
that he would swear for the Queen that she was a good woman.
Then said Mrs. Cosyn, ' Madam, why should any such matters
be spoken of ? ' ' Marry,' said the Queen, ' I bade him do so :
for I asked him why he did not go through with his marriage '
(to her cousin Margaret) ' and he made answer he would tarry
a time.' Then I said, ' You look for dead men's shoes, for if
aught came to the King, you would look to have me '. And he
said if he should have any such thought, he would his head
were off. And she said she could undo him if she would. And
therewith they fell out." [2]

The thought of that conversation filled the Queen with
panic when she remembered it. She saw again the look of
terror on Norreys' face. . . . But she continued speaking, as
if in some terrible dream.

" The Queen told Mrs. Cosyn she had ' spoken to Weston

because he did love her kinswoman' (the same Margaret), and loved not his wife; and he had made answer that he loved one in the Palace, better than both; and the Queen said, 'Who is that?' 'It is yourself,' he replied. And then she defied him."[3]

This death-dealing sleep-walker, in the dream that had been her life, had destroyed many things — the allegiance of the English Church to the Pope, the power of Wolsey. Because of her, indirectly, many men had come to their deaths. Now, in the delirium that preceded her own death, she destroyed Norreys and Weston. That speech cost them their heads.

She seems to have hated Mark Smeaton. When one of her watchers said, "Mark is the worst cherished in the Tower, for he weareth irons," the Queen said that was "because he was no gentleman". "He never was in my chamber," said she, "but at Winchester." And there she had sent for him to play upon the virginals, for there her lodging had been above that of the King. "And I never spake with him since, but upon Saturday before May Day, and then I found him standing in my chamber of presence. And I asked him why he was so sad. And he answered and said it was no matter. I said, 'You may not look to have me speak to you as I would do to a nobleman, because you are an inferior person.' 'No, no,' said he, 'a look sufficeth, and so fare you well.'"

Strype holds the curious opinion that this showed Smeaton "to be some haughty person, who thought the Queen showed him not respect enough, and so might take his opportunity to humble her, and revenge himself by this means on her, not thinking it would cost him his life".[4]

Often the mind of the doomed woman would dwell upon the past, and then, in a whisper, humbly and imploringly, or with anguish, hurriedly, as if there was no time to be lost, she would speak as if Mary was actually present, begging her forgiveness, craving one word to show that Mary had pardoned all she had suffered.

Sometimes her wanderings were those of some poor, harmless, hunted creature, longing for comfort. "I hear my lord my brother is here," said she. And when the Constable replied, "It is truth," "I am very glad we are so near together," said the woman who was soon to die. "Weston and Bryerton too," said the Constable, "and she made very glad countenance." (She must, I think, have been by now a little mad.) "I also said Mr. Page and Wyatt . . . then she said 'He — ha.'" [5]

Here the narrative breaks off. What does that "He — ha" mean? Was it laughter, or was it some communication that she was about to make, of which the words have been lost — blown away by time, or purposely destroyed?

The Constable was unable to understand her wanderings. "She hath asked my wife whether anybody makes their beads" — (this has been reported as "beds"). "And my wife answered, 'Nay, I warrant you'. Then the Queen said, 'They might make ballads well now, but there, no one but my Lord Rochford can do it'. 'Yes,' said my wife, 'Master Wyatt.' . . . 'True. My lord my brother will die.'"

Sometimes that poor ghost would weep, or pray, but at other times she was gay. One day she had a good dinner, and afterwards called for a supper, then, sending for Kingston, she went over, once more, her scene with the Commission, saying again, "But to be a Queen and so cruelly handled ! . . . But I think the King does it to prove me." And she laughed.

"I wish to God", she said to the waiting, whispering women sent to spy upon her, "I had my Bishops, for they would all go to the King for me. For I think the most part of England prayeth for me. And if I die, you shall see the greatest punishment for me within this seven years that ever came to England. And then, said she, shall I be in heaven. For I have done many good deeds in my life."

"Thus she spake no doubt in the confidence of her innocence ; And God's righteous and visible judgments for the most part, for shedding innocent blood. And indeed with the seventh year following happened a dreadful pestilence in London and many commotions and insurrections to the end of this reign." [6]

Her good deeds had been many. Wyatt could say, with truth, of this persecutor of the hapless Catherine and Mary that "each place felt that heavenly flame burning in her . . . no place leaving for vain flames, no time for idle thoughts". Her charities "amounted to fifteen hundred pounds at least, yearly, to be bestowed by the poor. . . . Her provisions of stocks for the poor in sundry needy parishes was very great. Out of her privy purse went not a little to like purposes . . . so as in three quarters of a year, her alms was summed to 14 or 15 thousand pounds " — a gigantic sum at that time.[7]

She suspected all about her ; but still the delirious words poured from her lips. She complained bitterly, saying she " thought it great unkindness in the King to set such about her as she never loved ; but the King wist what he did when he set two such women about her as my Lady Boleyn and Mrs. Cosyn. For they could tell her nothing of my lord her father, and nothing else. But that she defied them all. . . . But upon that, my Lady Boleyn . . . said to her, ' Such desire as you have had to such tales ' (tale-bearers) ' has brought you to this '. "[8]

Did she indeed hope that help would come from her Bishops ? Cranmer, who, according to himself, " owed more to her than to anyone ", after a visit to the bullying, hectoring Cromwell, knew that nothing could be done to save her, even if he im- perilled his own safety and the cause of the Reformed Church in England. He was a timid, though kindly creature, much in awe of those above him. " If the reports of the Queen be true," he wrote to the King, " they are only to her dishonour, not yours. I am clean amazed, for I never had better opinion of woman ; but I think your Highness would not have gone so far if she had not been culpable. . . . I loved her not a little for the love which I judged her to bear towards God and the Gospel. . . . I trust you will bear no less zeal to the Gospel than you did before, as your favour to the Gospel was not led by affection to her."

Then came a postscript, written a few hours afterwards — he having meanwhile spoken with the Lord Chancellor, Lord Oxford, and the Lord Chamberlain : " I am exceedingly sorry that such faults can be proved by the queen, as I heard of their relation ".[9]

Afterwards the Archbishop visited the Queen in her prison. It must have been a painful meeting. He had been her father's chaplain, and he had risen to be Archbishop through the Boleyn influence and because of his usefulness in the matter of the

divorce. He was godfather to Elizabeth. We know nothing
of what was said during that interview. All that is known is
that, trusting him, Anne seems to have admitted the existence
of some impediment to her marriage with the King, and that
the marriage could therefore be pronounced illegal, and Elizabeth
(even if Henry accepted her as his daughter) a bastard. . . . The
Earl of Northumberland had refused to admit there was a pre-
contract between the Queen and himself, therefore some other
pretext must be found. Cranmer had proved his usefulness
once again.

After that interview, the Queen believed — possibly because
she may have been promised her life if she would admit to an
impediment — that she would be banished to a convent instead
of being condemned to death. But that belief did not last long.
Before the day of the trial, she knew, not only that she must die,
but that nothing in all her life, no pure happiness, no natural
impulse, remained unfouled by the hands of her enemies. Even
her natural love for her brother had been stained by that un-
speakable touch.

There was no reason left why she should wish to preserve
her broken life.

The trial began on the 15th of May, the accused men being,
besides Smeaton, Norreys, Rochford, and Weston — Bryerton
(one of the King's captains), Sir Richard Page, and others.

Those who must die with the Queen were Smeaton, Rochford, Norreys, Weston, and Bryerton.

The following charges were made :

" That whereas Queen Anne has been the wife of Henry
the Eighth for three years and more, she, despising her marriage
and entertaining malice against the King, and following daily
her frail and carnal lust, did falsely and traitorously procure by
means of base conversations, touchings, gifts, and other infamous
incitations, divers of the King's daily and familiar servants to
be her adulterers and concubines, so that several of the King's
servants yielded to her vile provocations : viz. 6th October
25 Henry VIII (1533) " (one month after the birth of Elizabeth)
" at Westminster, and divers days before and after, she procured,
by sweet words, kisses, touches, and otherwise, Henry Norreys.

. . . That the Queen 3rd December, 25 Hen. VIII, procured and incited William Brereton, Esqre, one of the gentlemen of the King's privy chamber, to have illicit intercourse with her ; and that the act was committed at Westminster, 25 December : 26 Hen. VIII . . . That the Queen, 8th May, 26 Hen. VIII, procured Francis Weston, one of the gentlemen of the King's privy chamber, to have illicit intercourse with her ; and that the act was committed at Westminster, 20 May : 26 Hen. VIII, then, most horrible charge of all : That the Queen, 2nd of November : 27 Hen. VIII (1535), by the means therein stated, procured George Boleyn, knight, Lord Rochford, her own natural brother . . . against the commands of Almighty God, and all laws human and divine." (These were but a few of the dates mentioned with regard to all the accused.)

" Furthermore," the charge continues, they (the accused men), " being thus inflamed by carnal love of the Queen, and having become very jealous of each other, did, in order to secure her affections, satisfy her inordinate desires ; and that the Queen was equally jealous of the Lord Rochford and other of the before-mentioned traitors ; and she would not allow them to show any familiarity with any other woman, without her exceeding displeasure and indignation ; and that on the 27th day of November, 27 Hen. VIII, and other days, at Westminster, she gave them gifts and great rewards, to inveigle them to her will.

" Furthermore, that the Queen, and other of the said traitors, jointly and severally, 31st October, 27 Hen. VIII, and at various times before and after, compassed and imagined the King's death ; And that the Queen had frequently promised to marry some one of the traitors, whenever the King should depart this life, affirming she never would love the King in her heart.

" Furthermore, that the King, having within a short time before become acquainted with the before-mentioned abominable crimes, vices, and treasons against himself, took such inward displeasure and heaviness, especially for his said Queen's malice and adultery, that certain harms and perils have befallen his royal body."

Nothing, except the giant diatribe in which King Lear pours scorn upon the race of women, can give the likeness of such a being as that into which this light native of the summer was transformed :

> But to the girdle doe the gods inherit,
> Beneath is all the Fiends.
> There's hell, there's darkness, there is the sulphurous pit ;
> Burning, scalding, stench, consumption, Fye, fye, fie.

The Queen was in addition accused of being a poisoner. . . . It was said that she had given Norreys a locket — probably a receptacle of poison to bring about the death of the late Queen Catherine.

" The detail ", said Froude (Henry VIII), " was given of acts and conversations stretching over a period of two years and more ; and either there was evidence for these things, or there was none. If there was evidence, it must have been close, elaborate, and minute ; if there was none, these judges, these juries and noblemen, were the accomplices of the King in a murder perhaps the most revolting that was ever committed.

" It may be thought that the evidence was pieced together in the secrecy of the cabinet ; that the juries found their bills on a case presented to them by the Council. This would transfer the infamy to a higher stage ; but if we try to imagine how the council proceeded to such a business, we shall not find it an easy task. The Council, at least, could not have been deceived. The evidence, whatever it was, must have been examined by them." And he enquires " Can we believe that Cromwell would have invented that dark indictment — Cromwell who was, and who remained till his death, the dearest friend of Latimer ? Or the Duke of Norfolk, the veteran who had won his spurs at Flodden ? Or the Duke of Suffolk and Sir William Fitzwilliam, the Wellington and the Nelson of the 16th century ? Scarcely among the picked scoundrels of Newgate could men be found for such work ; and shall we believe it of men like these ? It is to me impossible. Yet, if it was done at all, it was done by those four ministers."

Froude then gives the names of the jurors, saying, " I am thus particular, because, if that indictment was unjust, it stamps their memory with eternal infamy ; and with the judges, the commissioners, the privy council, the king, with every living person who was a party, active or passive, to so enormous a calumny, they must be remembered with shame for ever ".

That the jury, the judges, and in all probability the King, thought the Queen guilty seem indisputable ; but " the lord mayor, who, as chief judge in the civic court of judicature, had been accustomed to weigh evidences and pronounce judgments ", was present at her arraignment, and said, subsequently, that " he could not observe anything in the proceedings against her, but that they were resolved to make an occasion to get rid of her ".[10]

Whence came the evidence against her ? " This is an entry ", says Miss Strickland, " made by Sir John Spilman, in his private note-book, supposed to have been written on the bench when he sat as one of the judges of Norris, Weston, Brereton, and Smeaton." . . . " As for the evidence of the matter, it was discovered by the lady Wingfield, who had been a servant to the queen, and becoming suddenly infirm, before her death did swear the matter to one of her . . ." Here the page is torn off.[11]

We know that, according to his own account, Cromwell had set himself to " fantasier et conspirer " the affair. But it is possible that, in his own view, he was but setting a legitimate trap for a guilty woman who had hitherto escaped a just punishment. The present writer believes her to have been condemned, in reality, for sins and faults for which she was not arraigned — for her boldness and un-Queen-like demeanour, her loud laughter, the spell she cast over the husband of another woman — for her insolence and cruelty to Catherine and Mary, her interference with the life of the nation.

The Queen and her brother were charged separately, the others accused in a body. The cowardly, bombastic old man whose son and daughter were to die, was present at the trial of those who were to suffer with them, but not at their own. Here, however, the frightful Lady Rochford, to whose vicious life the presence of her husband was so inconvenient, brought still one further accusation, at first kept secret, to make his death, and that of his sister, certain. Then Rochford, knowing their lives were forfeit, repeated loudly in court this accusation that Cromwell had hoped to keep from the people — the assertion made by his abominable wife that Anne told her the King was impotent as a result of his disease.

From that moment, all hope was dead.

But there was still one formality to be gone through. Those about to die must have sentence passed upon them.

The Duke of Norfolk, although he had hated his niece because of her arrogance and insolence, broke into tears as he pronounced the sentence. The Earl of Northumberland, who had once loved the Queen, was seized with illness before the moment of her condemnation came, and left the court.

Anne Queen of England was sentenced to be beheaded or burned at the King's pleasure, — a sentence that she heard without shrinking, saying, according to Chapuys' account, that she held herself " pour toute saluée de la mort ". " I confess," she said, " I have had jealous fancies and suspicions of the King, which I had not discretion and wisdom enough to conceal at all times. But God knows, and is my witness, that I never sinned against him in any other way. Think not I say this in the hope to prolong my life. . . . As for my brother, and those others who are unjustly condemned, I would willingly suffer many deaths to deliver them ; but since I see it so pleases the King, I shall willingly accompany them in death, with the assurance that I shall live an endless life with them in peace." [12]

She then saluted her judges, and left the court.

The witch-Queen, who, by means of her spells, had entangled the King in a false marriage with her, the usurper Queen who had brought so many great and revered men to their downfall or death, was spared a death by fire. She, and the others (with the exception of Smeaton, who was hanged), were beheaded.

On the 19th of May, four days after their trial, Rochford and the four other condemned men were executed, without, however, undergoing the worst horrors of the death for treason.

" The Concubine ", Chapuys told his master, " saw them executed from the Tower, to aggravate her grief."

She was told that she was to die on the morning succeeding the day on which she had seen that appalling sight from her window.

So, she told herself, her grief, her terror, would soon be over.

Oh, why had she not died in the plague of 1528, the sweating sickness, when she and her father had been stricken? In that plague, whose causes were, it was believed, partly astrological, partly the result of fear, and of the filthy state of the streets, if one died it was like the vanishing of a meteor in the early autumn mists — so soon was one gathered away. Two ladies would be standing talking — one would turn red and fiery, and one yellow, like two evil comets. Then black spots would appear; their voices would fade in the midst of a word, and they would fall dead. "One had a little pain in the head and heart," the French Ambassador du Bellay wrote, "then all is over." But this pain in the head and heart would not cease until the head was taken from the body.

For that she must wait still another day, for the executioner had not yet arrived.

She had spent the night expecting death in the morning, but then was told by her attendants that she was not to die till noon. Sending for Kingston, in a broken voice she spoke to him of the horror and terror she endured through the delay. She had hoped, she said, to be past her pain.

The Keeper of the Tower tried to comfort her, telling her she would have no pain, for all was over so quickly. She replied, yes, she had a little neck. The people who had found a vile name for the late Queen, would find one also for her. She would be called "Queen Lackhead" — and overcome by the waiting, and by the frightful scene she had witnessed from her window, she shrieked with laughter. The Constable, much astonished, told Cromwell: "I have seen many men and women executed, and that they have been in great sorrow, and to my knowledge this lady hath much joy and pleasure in death".

Still the executioner did not come . . . all the rest of that day and the succeeding night, she must endure her agony. Sometimes she would fall on her knees and pray. Sometimes she would talk, in her wandering way, with her ladies.

At last, at nine o'clock next morning, the Constable told the Queen the hour of her release had come.

Bacon declared that, just before she went to execution, she sent the King this message " by a messenger faithful and generous

as she supposed, who was one of the King's privy chamber :
' Commend me to his grace, and tell him he hath ever been
constant in his career of advancing me ; from a private gentle-
woman he made me a marchioness, from a marchioness a queen,
and now he hath left me a higher degree of honour, he gives
my innocency the crown of martyrdom '. But the messenger
durst not carry this to the King, then absorbed in a new passion.
Yet tradition hath truly transmitted it to posterity."

The family of Bacon were intimately connected with the
Court ; Sir Antony Cooke, his uncle, being tutor to Edward VI ;
his aunt and mother were both in the service of Queen Mary,
and, says Agnes Strickland, " all these persons must have heard
the facts from witnesses ".

Now in her gown of black damask, that had no collar, with
her hair, tied up so that it could not hinder the stroke of the
axe, hidden under the coif with the great pearls, she crept into
the courtyard of the Tower.

There, fingering her neck, and looking behind her, from
time to time, to where the executioners waited, she said a few
words. . . .

" Good Christian people, I am come hither to die, according
to law, for by the law I am judged to die, and therefore will
speak nothing against it." [13] " I am come hither to accuse no
man, nor to speak anything of that whereof I am accused. . . .
But I am come here only to die, and thus to yield myself humbly
unto the will of my lord the king. I pray God to save the king,
and send him long to reign over you, for a gentler or more
merciful prince was there never. To me he was ever a good
and gentle sovereign lord. If any person will meddle with
my cause, I require them to judge the best." . . .

The executioners advanced, and she who had talked, in her
life, too much and too lightly, whispered, " Oh God have pity
on my soul " . . . then spoke no more.

" No person ", wrote Chapuys, in a momentary compassion
for the woman he had so passionately hated, " ever showed greater
willingness to die." He added that a lady who had charge of her
" sent to tell me in great secrecy that the Concubine, before
and after receiving the Sacrament, affirmed to her, on the

damnation or salvation of her soul, that she had never been unfaithful to the King — 'n'avais jamais méfaicte de son corps
envers ce roy'."

From the morning of the Queen's arrest, during the time
of her trial and after her condemnation, the King and the Court
indulged in balls and feasts. Each night, down the long river
that had seemed, before, as quiet as the waters of Lethe, the
King's barge floated, and the music from it was carried by the
small spring wind.

Sometimes the Children of the Chapel would sing a work
by the late William Cornish, once Master of the King's Music :

> You and I and Amyas,
> Amyas and you and I
> To the greenwood must we go ; alas —
> You and I, my life, and Amyas . . .

the sound floating, perhaps, to the window, not so far away, of
the woman who no more would to the greenwood go ; — the
musicians would play " Ah Robin, gentle Robin ", " Lady
Carey's Dompe " — a dompe or dump being a slow dance —
or that beautiful strange song composed by the King himself,
" O western wind when wilt thou blow " — the sound itself
being like that of a dark soft wind blowing among the flowering
buds of a tree in some warm corner of a garden — or " The
Dargason or Sedany ", " Flaunting Two ", " Mopsy's Tune ",
" Shall I go walk the woods so wild ", " Lady Wingfield's
Rounde ", Sellinger's Round ", — or the dance-tunes recently
come out of Scotland, " All Christian Men's Dance ", " Long
Flat Foot of Garioch ", " The Lamb's Wind ", " Leaves Green ",
" The Bace of Vorragar ", " Shake a Trot ", " The Loch of
Slene ", " The Alman Hey ", " Rank at the Root ", and " The
Dead Days ".

On a certain dawn, when the skies were beginning to turn
green, and the green star of Venus shone, the Court ladies might
have been seen leaving the palace of the Bishop of Carlisle, at
the water-side, and entering their barges, for the Bishop had
given a great supper-party for the King, and this had lasted late.

The green light glittered faintly upon gowns of such hues as ruby, crane, drake, " flybert ", " goselinge ", horseflesh, Isabella (a pale yellow), turtle, and willow. . . . Then, under the shadow of the trees, as they passed beneath them toward the steps leading down to the water, you saw that their faces and bodies were changed as by the grave — that " in their curious antic-woven garments, they imitate and mock the worms and adders that must eat them ", — and that " Time's sickle had been burst in twain to make their periwigs more elevated arches of . . . the pride of their hearts, like the moth, lies closely shrouded amid the threads of that apparel ".

Like their lost mistress, " those crystal countenances ", under the network of shadows cast by the branches, " seemed masquelike, caul-visarded with venemous crawling worms ".[14]

The last lady embarked — the last sound died away.

At that supper-party the Bishop was, privately, much shocked by the King telling him he had long foreseen what would be the end of his wife. Taking a book out of his doublet, Henry showed the Bishop a tragedy he had written on the subject. " You never saw prince nor man ", Chapuys told the Chancellor Granville, " who made greater show of his horns, or bore them more pleasantly. I leave you to imagine why."

At the time of the trial the King was at Hampton Court, and the future Queen of England, the modest and silent Jane Seymour, was at the house of Sir Nicholas Carew, some seven miles from London. But soon the distance that lay between the King and his beloved seemed too great, and she was removed to a house on the Thames only a mile from the Court. Here she lived in great state, as if she were already Queen ; and here it was that the King, faithful to his promise, sent Hell's Vicar, Sir Francis Bryane, cousin to the condemned woman, to tell Jane that the mistress she had supplanted was to die.

There were then but a few days to wait before virtue was rewarded. Soon after nine o'clock on Friday the 20th of May, the cannon at the Tower boomed out the news that the Queen of England had been beheaded ; and at this signal the King, dressed in white as a sign of mourning, stepped into his barge, and went to spend the rest of the day with his future Queen.

As he brushed through the green branches on his short walk from the barge to the house, he must have looked as Catherine had seen him, one May Day, when he was young and had risen "early in the morning, to fetch may or hawthorn boughs, his grace being richly apparelled, his knights, squires, and gentlemen being attired in white satin, his yeoman and guard in white sarcanet ; in this manner went every man with his bow and arrows shooting into the wood, and in similar guise returned again to the Court, each person with a green bough in his cap ".[15]

Now, too, the white attire of the King was wet with dew.

At six o'clock the next morning, Jane Seymour left her house secretly, entered her barge, and went to join the King at Hampton Court. Here, shortly afterwards, in the presence of a few courtiers, the marriage took place. Some days passed, then the marriage was made public, and the dead woman's supplanter took her place as Queen.

NOTES TO CHAPTER NINE

[1] Thomas Dekker, *Jests to Make You Merrie*.
[2] Kingston to Cromwell.
[3] Kingston to Cromwell.
[4] Strype, *Memorials*.
[5] Kingston to Cromwell.
[6] Strype, *Memorials*.
[7] Wyatt, *Memoirs of Queen Anne Boleyn*.
[8] Strype, *Memorials*.
[9] Burnet, *History of the Reformation*, vol. i.
[10] Agnes Strickland, *Anne Boleyn*. (Lives of the Queens of England.)
[11] Burnet, *History of the Reformation*, vol. i.
[12] The Account of Crispin, Lord of Milherve, an eye-witness.
[13] Hall's *Chronicle* ; Wyatt, *Memoir of Queen Anne Boleyn*.
[14] Thomas Nashe, *Christ's Teares over Jerusalem*.
[15] Holinshed's *Chronicle*, i. 556.

Chapter Ten

THAT poor ghost, with her gay light laughing movements bringing down doom upon herself and so many grave and wise men — that ghost, light as the gay young Jack-a-dandy of summer dancing on the ceilings and walls of the nursery-palace at Hunsdon, had gone. Nothing remained of her, now, but a mouldering body laid deep in a nameless grave in the Tower — the head that had held so many summer thoughts, separated from the body that had once danced so lightly. Each year a little gay ghost of gold would come back again, creeping through the windows and doors of the nursery-palace, but it would not bring in its train that other ghost of a past and heedless summer.

The child of that ghost would never, in all her long life, speak the name of her who lay in that blood-stained grave. Her name, the fact that it had once been part of a living reality, must be kept in silence for ever, like some appalling and obscene secret. Yet through all the life of that child, until she was an old woman, the unnamed ghost, and the phantom of the supposed sin, would rise from its grave and come, in the warmth of the sun and the fire of the full moon, bringing the chill of its death and the real or imagined fever of lust that not even death could assuage, to stand between Elizabeth and happiness, or to add its own horror to a later horror, its blood to blood that was still wet.

Years after her own youth had gone, the daughter of that ghost wrote to the only man she had ever loved — the man whom she loved as dearly as she loved England, though she renounced marriage with him, and all the happiness and hope of her personal life, for England's sake : " Rob, I am afraid you will suppose by my wanderings that a midsummer moon hath taken possession of my brains ! " For one moment she re-lived the days when it was summer, and happiness seemed near — then that shade advanced, and the midsummer moon was blotted

out. She would see, for a moment, the face of love. Then
suddenly in its place was a skull . . . the blood of youth turned
cold under the freezing breath.

That horror after the execution of Mary Queen of Scots, —
those floods of tears, that refusal to eat and inability to sleep.
. . . What did Elizabeth see, as she stared before her ? Two
heads, not one, lying in the dust — a head with greying hair,
and a young head with long black hair and great slanting eyes.
And beside the blood that was newly shed, was an old stain of
what had once been life.

But when that life was spilt, Elizabeth was a little child,
not three years old, and now she who, a few weeks after her
birth, was proclaimed heiress-presumptive to the throne of
England, in default of male children — the child for whose
sake Princess Mary was disinherited, was, in her turn, pronounced
a bastard. And poor Lady Bryane, governess-in-ordinary, or
" lady mistress ", to the royal children, was distracted. Lady
Bryane was a step-sister to the Duke of Norfolk, and to the
mother of Anne Boleyn, — she was a member of Lord Berners'
family. The wife of one Lord Berners left him for " the raggle-
taggle gypsies — O ", and was celebrated for that reason in a
song. But this daughter of the ancient house had no addiction
to gypsies. Nor had she any likeness to her riotous, yet sly, son,
Sir Francis Bryane, Hell's Vicar. She was a being like the old
woman who " sate under the dove-house wall " ; and to her
an earthquake was only the shaking of the dove-house as the
doves flew out. Juliet might have been her nursling, as well as
Elizabeth. Now Lady Bryane, in her feathery white gown that
was tight over her bosom, with her white cap tied under her
chin, and her round old eyes full of perplexity, was at her wits'
end. Nobody could tell her anything, or give her any instructions, excepting Mr. Shelton, whom one supposes to have been
the son of Princess Mary's *governante* (for the establishments of
the two disinherited Princesses were quartered together at
Hunsdon). — And his instructions were unwelcome. Lady
Bryane did *not* expect to be taught her duty by Mr. Shelton :
but she did not know if she was head of her Grace's household,
or if Mr. Shelton had been put above her ! She did not know

if her lady grace might still be called her lady grace, or how she must be addressed!

To whom could she turn for advice? Why of course she must write to Lord Cromwell, the Lord Privy Seal; for had he not promised, on his last visit to Hunsdon, to help her if, at any time, she was in a difficulty? . . .

Lord Cromwell . . . what a charming man! How amiable, how appreciative of one's efforts to make everything run smoothly! Understanding perfectly that it is very difficult to work with people who have new-fashioned (and to *some* people, almost *unpleasant*) ideas! Lord Cromwell was interested in small matters, knowing it is the small matters, and not the big, that count in the long run! He was not like some people, always in a hurry, impatient of details, and inattentive when you spoke to them. On the contrary, he was always laughing, always cheerful, and ready to give advice. He would be walking along a gallery of the Palace, his face heavy with thought. You would stop him, and he would give you his attention at once, looking at you with that sideways, roguish glance. Ah, there was a man you could trust! *He* would never approve of the disinheriting of that poor soul's child — nay, I warrant you! You could not find a more straightforward man than Lord Cromwell: you knew where you were with him. And every complaint made to the King's servants, all the business of the country would, in time, reach him — every perplexity must be laid before him.

The landscape, for instance, was already darkened by shadows called Egyptians, or gypsies (the bane of a future Lord Berners) — and in a little time from now Lord Cromwell would be asked what was to be done with certain of those shadows, who had been netted in Romney Marsh, and who had shown the authorities a patent of the King under the Great Seal, given to John Nany, Knight of Little Egypt, and his company. The Lord Privy Seal must deal not only with Sir John Nany, and these other dusky personages, thieving, creeping under hedges, and demanding to have their palms crossed with silver — but, also, with the plea of James Granada, an esquire of the King's stable, to be allowed to export 300 tuns of beer; he must decide the exact sum to be paid as a reward to an old woman for bringing back Cutte, the King's spaniel, when he ran away.

With these matters Lord Cromwell dealt ; as (a few years later, just before his own execution) he must deal with the affair of John Harrydance, " the inspired bricklayer ", who insisted upon preaching from his open window, between ten and twelve o'clock on a hot August night, to the great annoyance of his neighbours the King's servants, — and with the complaints of the permanently furious, half-mad Duchess of Norfolk.

Lord Cromwell listened to all pleas and complaints, and having listened, he would laugh, and soothe the complainant. He would also receive, gratefully and charmingly, any small present that came his way — a gold whistle and a gold toothpick from a poor widow — a fat crane and a fat swan for a winter feast.

Remembering that amiability, and Lord Cromwell's accessible nature, Lady Bryane, her head held a little on one side, her quill scratching the paper, began a letter to him :

" My lord," she wrote, — " after my most bounden duty, I recommend me to your good lordship, beseeching you to be good lord to me. Now is the greatest need that ever was, for it hath pleased God to take from me them that was my greatest comfort in the world, to my great heaviness." (Lady Bryane paused for a moment, wiped her eyes, then continued :) " Jesu have mercy upon her soul. And now I am succourless, and as a redeles [?] creature. But for the great trust which I have in the King's grace and your good lordship, for now in you I put my whole trust of comfort in this world.

" My lord, when your lordship was last here, it pleased you to say that I should not mistrust the King's Grace, nor your lordship. Which word was more comfort to me than I can ever write, as God knoweth. And now it boldeneth me to show you my poor mind. My lord, when my lady Marie's grace was born, it pleased the King's grace to [appoint] me lady mistress and made [sic] me a Baroness, and so I have been a [governess] to the children his grace have had since.

" Now it is so, my lady Elizabeth is put from that degree

she was afore : and what degree she is at now, I know not, but by hearsay. Therefore, I know not how to order her, nor myself, nor none of hers that I have the rule of ; that is, her women and her grooms : beseeching you to be good lord to my lady and to all hers ; and that she may have some raiment, for she hath neither gown, nor kirtall " (slip), " nor petticoat, nor no manner of linnen, nor foresmocks " (pinafores), " nor kerchief, nor rails " (nightgowns), " nor mofelers " (mob-caps), " nor biggens " (night-caps). " All these her grace mostake " (must have). " I have driven off as long as I can, that, to my troth I cannot drive it any longer : beseeching you, my lord, that you will see that her grace may have that is needful for her, as my trust is you will do. . . . My lord, Mr. Shelton says he is master of this house. What fashion that shall be, I know not. For I have not seen it afore. My lord, ye be so honourable yourself, and every man reporteth your lordship hath honour, that I trust your lordship will see the house honourably ordered. . . . And if it please you that I may know what your order is, and if it be not performed I shal certify your Lordship of it. For I fear me it will be hardely performed. But if the head of —— knew what honour meaneth, it will be the better ordered : if not, it will be hard to bring it to pass.

" My lord, Mr. Shelton would have my lady Elizabeth to dine and supp every day at the board of estate. Alas ! my lord, it is not meet for a child of that age to keep such rule yet. I promise you, my lord, I dare not take it upon me to keep her in health, and she keep that rule. For there she shall see divers meats and fruits and wine : which would be hard for me to restrain her grace from it. Ye know, my lord, there is no place of correction there, and she is yet too young to correct greatly, I know well and " (if) " she be there, I shall neither bring her up to the King's grace's honour, nor hers, nor to her health, nor my poor honesty. Wherefore I show your lordship this my desire : beseeching you, my lord, that my lady may have a mess of meat to her own lodging, with a good dish or two, that is meet for her grace to eat of : and the reversion of the mess shall satisfy all her women, a gentleman usher, and a groom, which ben eleven persons on her side. . . .

" God knoweth my lady hath great pain with her great teeth, and they come very slowly forth : and causeth me to suffer her grace to have her will more than I would. I trust to God, an her teeth were well graft, to have her grace after another fashion than she is yet : so as I trust the King's grace shall have great comfort in her grace. For she is as toward a child, and as gentle of conditions, as any in my life. Jesu preserve her grace. As for a day or two at a high time, or when it shall please the King's grace to have her set abroad, I trust so to endeavour me, that she shall do as shall be to the King's honour and hers : and then after to take her ease again.

" I think Mr. Shelton will not be content with this. He may " (must ?) " not know it is my desire ; but that it is the King's pleasure and yours it should be so. Good my lord, have my lady's grace and us that be your poor servants in your remembrance. And your lordship shall have an hearty prayer by the grace of Jesu.

" From Hunsdon, with the evil hand of her that is your daily bedeswoman

Margaret Bryane."

There is no date.

. . . Lady Bryane, with a nervous start, put down the letter. . . . Could that be Mr. Shelton, come to spy upon her ? No, it was only Elizabeth Candysshe, one of her grace's women, going to a cupboard in the next room.

Ubiquitous, interfering Mr. Shelton ! . . . His clothes looked always as if they were a suit of armour, but he, himself, was like a ghost inside them — a thin ghost with a beard as grey and as dry as rosemary, and a bonnet worn in exact imitation of his grace's way. You never knew where he was, for in spite of that armoured appearance he could move as quickly as a spring wind, that enters a room and steals something away before you realise the thief has come or gone. What business had Mr. Shelton to come into the nurseries at all hours ? Let him stay in his own apartments, and run the household accounts ! But unhappily he was determined to rule the nursery-palace down to the smallest detail. Not only did he give orders to the wood-carriers bringing wood to her grace's nurseries, but he interfered downstairs in the still-rooms, telling the maids how to distil the sweet water of roses, lavender, mace, cloves, cypress roots, yellow sanders, benzoin, storax, calamine, musk ; the "Water of Buradge" (borage), "Water of Fumitory, Water of Brakes" (ferns), "Water of Columbyns, Water of Okyn Lufe" (oak-leaves), "Water of Harts' Tongue, Water of Draggons" (snapdragon), "Water of Parcelly" (parsley), "Water of Walnut Leefs, Water of Primeroses, Water of Saidge" (sage), "Water of Sorrel, Water of Red Mynt, Water of Betany, Water of Cowslips, Water of Tantelyon" (dandelion), "Water of Fennel, Water of Scabious, Water of Elder Flowers, Water of Marigolds, Water of Wilde Tansey, Water of Wormewode, Water of Woodbind, Water of Endyff, and Water of Hawsse" (hawthorn flowers).[1]

Mr. Shelton interfered with the making of all these, and with the distillation of King Henry's Perfume, whose recipe is given in The Lady's Closet : "of composed water, six spoonful, as much of rose water, a quarter of an ounce of fine sugar, two grains of musk, two grains of ambergris, two of civet, boil softly together, and the house will smell of musk".

Yes, Mr. Shelton was a household revolutionary. Taking up the letter again, Lady Bryane re-read the sentences referring to her grace's appearance in public. . . . Elizabeth was an odd child, with a will as resistless as fire. What she wanted to do, she did, and there were moments when her face, for all its babyish roundness, bore a strange resemblance to that of her formidable father.

Lady Bryane had been in charge of the baby from the time of the christening. She superintended the weaning of the Princess, an affair so important that it was discussed with the Ministers of State, as we shall see from this passage in one of Sir William Powlet's letters to Cromwell :

"The King's grace, well considering the letter directed to you from my lady Bryane and other of my lady Princess's officers, his grace with the assent of the Queen's grace, hath fully determined the weaning of my lady princess to be done with all diligence !

"From Sarum. October 9."

Immediately after this "nursery event of state", as Miss Strickland called it, the King "exercised his paternal care in seeking a suitable consort for the royal weanling". The husband chosen was the baby Duc d'Angoulême, the third son of Francis I. But King Henry insisted that if a betrothal was to take place, the little Prince must be educated in England (in order that he might be a suitable consort for the future Queen), and that he must hold the Duchy of Angoulême independently of France. The demands of the French King were as exorbitant, and were tinged with insolence. It would be necessary, said Gontier, who had been sent to England (as we have seen) to arrange the betrothal, that Elizabeth should be made perfectly sure of her rank, as the Duc d'Angoulême could not marry a woman whose social and political status was in doubt.[2]

Angered by this, Henry replied that Elizabeth was the undoubted heir to the throne ; but that, if Francis felt any qualms, he had only to force the Pope to recall the sentence given by Pope Clement, and to declare the marriage with Catherine to have been null from the beginning.

These were not the only difficulties. The dowry Elizabeth would bring to the son of the French King was discussed. And Francis demanded "no less than the renunciation by Henry of the title of King of France, and the extinction of all pensions, arrears, or payments which the French were by treaty bound to pay to him — a sum of about 120,000 crowns a year".

At this exorbitant claim, Henry broke into a fury, and "could not", said Friedmann, "for some time recover his equanimity. In the end, he said that 50,000 crowns of perpetual pension he was ready to give up, but the 60,000 which were to be paid him personally during life, he would not relinquish."

The Council went still further than the King ; they refused to give up a single crown of the pension. . . .

The betrothal therefore did not take place.

Cromwell had made another suggestion to Chapuys : that the baby Elizabeth might be betrothed to Philip, son of the Emperor, but, said Friedmann,[3] "brazen-faced as he was, even Cromwell did not dare to press this scheme, and Chapuys contemptuously ignored all references to it".

Lady Bryane was in charge during the two months which the new-born Princess spent at Greenwich before her journey to Hatfield, and her subsequent long residence at the Bishop's Palace in Chelsea. . . . Those days at Greenwich had been happy . . . the Queen was in a gay mood, and there was the fun of choosing caps and ribbons for the baby. . . . Ah, how well Lady Bryane remembered the day when a royal barge brought from London to Greenwich a woman milliner to measure the baby for a white satin cap with a caul of gold, and a purple satin cap ; and the very same morning the Queen's grace had chosen the crimson satin and crimson fringe for the Princess's cradle, and some green ribbon to garnish a pair of clavichords.[4]

Poor thing, poor thing ! . . . Lady Bryane sighed. That green ribbon was still in existence, but now it had grown dusty.

The time at the Bishop's Palace at Chelsea was pleasant ; eventually the King had built a Palace there, for the air suited the baby ; and of this Palace Lady Bryane's husband was made Keeper. . . . One day, in a later summer, when the Princess was just able to walk, she planted, with great ceremony, a mulberry tree, in the gardens of the Palace.

Now this poor child, once heiress to the throne of England, had been pronounced, in Parliament, and by her own god-father Archbishop Cranmer, a bastard, like her sister Mary, who had been disinherited for her sake. Lady Bryane had also brought up Mary from her babyhood, and loved her tenderly, seeing her in the light in which an Italian contemporary, Pollini, viewed this poor and uncared-for being, whose character, naturally of great goodness, was already overshadowed by the doom of madness that had engulfed her aunt, Queen Juana of Castile, and that hung over many other members of her mother's family. " Mary ", said the Italian, " was small, fragile, and of a singularly beautiful complexion, but of a very different kind from that of her father ; when she was a girl, she was much celebrated for her beauty, but the troubles she underwent in her father's reign, faded her charms prematurely, though she was far from being ugly. Her face was short, her forehead very large, her eyes dark and lustrous, and remarkably touching when she fixed them on anyone."

From the moment of Elizabeth's birth, " it was ordered [5] that the true Princess should not be so called, and her lackeys were deprived of their gold-embroidered coats, which they wore with her device, in place of which the arms of the King alone have been put on them. . . . Like the wise and virtuous Princess she is, she takes matters patiently, and has written a comforting letter to the Queen her mother."

Later, " in consequence of the King's resolution and order as to the respective treatment of the Princess and of his bastard daughter . . . the latter was, three days since, taken to a house seventeen miles from this city ; and although there was a better and a shorter route thither, yet, for the sake of pompous solemnity, and the better to impress upon the people the idea of her being the true Princess . . . the King's bastard daughter, and her suite, composed of . . . noblemen . . . were made to traverse this city. On the ensuing morning, the Duke of Norfolk went to the Princess, and signified her father's pleasure that she should . . . enter the service of his bastard daughter, whom the Duke deliberately, and in her presence, called Princess of Wales." (This title was used, by Chapuys, by mistake.) " Upon which Princess Mary replied, ' That is a title that belongs to me by right, and to no one else '. . . . The Duke said to her that he had not gone thither to dispute, but to see the King's wishes carried out, and his commands executed, namely, that she should be removed to the house taken for the bastard. . . .

" Upon which the Princess, seeing that all her arguments . . . would be of no avail, asked for half an hour in which to retire to her private chamber ; where she remained . . . occupied in drawing up the protest whereof I once gave her the words. Thus, should she be in any way compelled by force or persuaded by deceit to renounce her rights, marry against her will, or enter a cloister, no prejudice should result to her hereafter.

" When she came out of her room, the Princess said to the Duke : ' Since such is my father's wish, it is not for me to disobey his injunctions ; but I beg you to intercede with him that the services of many well-deserving and trusty officers of my household may be rewarded, and one year's wages at least given them.' After this, she asked the Duke how many of her own servants she would be allowed to retain and take with her. The answer was that as she would find plenty of servants to attend on her where she was going, no great train of followers was needed. Accordingly, the Princess set out on her journey, accompanied only by very few of her household. Her governess (the Countess of Salisbury), daughter of the late Duke of Clarence, a very honourable and virtuous lady, if there be one in England, — offered, I hear, to serve the Princess at her own cost, with a good and honourable train of servants, but her offers were not accepted ; nor will they ever be ; for were the said lady to remain by the Princess, they would no longer be able to execute their bad designs, which are evidently either to cause her to die of grief, or in some other way, or else to compel her to renounce her rights, marry some low fellow, or let her fall a prey to lust, so that they may have a pretext for disinheriting her and submitting her to all manner of bad treatment.[6]

" When the Princess," Chapuys continues, " who was taken away with only two attendants, arrived where the King's bastard was, the Duke asked her whether she would not go and pay her respects to the Princess. She replied that she knew no other Princess in England except herself, and that the daughter of Madame de Penebrok [sic] had no such title ; but it was true that since the King her father acknowledged her to be his, she might call her ' sister ' as she called the Duke of Richmond ' brother '. . . . The Duke asked her what word he should carry to the King, to which she replied, ' Nothing else, excepting that his daughter, the Princess, begged his blessing '. And when he said he would not carry such a message, she told him, curtly, he might leave it, and after protesting several times that what she did at the King's command should not be to her prejudice, she retired to weep in her chamber, as she does constantly."

Now, Lady Bryane, thinking of her two unfortunate nurslings, wiped her eyes, shaking her head mournfully. Then, turning in her chair, she saw the newly disinherited Elizabeth standing beside her. The Princess, so young she was barely able to keep on her feet, buried her head, which was the colour of a lion cub's, in Lady Bryane's bosom, and began to cry. First, she cried with a kind of angry roar — because she was furious with the rebellious tooth that would not come from its hiding-place — the tooth that defied her, and would not let her have her own way — and because she was in pain. Then her tears fell more quietly, as if she were just a sad little girl, — not a Princess who must not be contradicted, but a little child in a world that would never understand her, — lonely and unloved.

Lady Bryane, picking her up, kissed her with a kind of hungry violence.

What are you to do with a being which even in childhood has an alien greatness, the look of the lion — and who is doomed to a history like that of the sun, a life of grandeur and loneliness and all-seeing wisdom.

But Lady Bryane's thoughts were not of destiny. A toothache was in progress, and the toothache must be dealt with. Old ways are often the best. First, one must seek the cause of the trouble. According to an early authority, Trevisa, " Wormes breede in the cheke teethe . . . and this is knowen by itchynge and tyckelinge and continyall digging and thyrlynge" (boring?). " Wormes of the teethe ben slayne with myrrhe and opium ".[7] . . . A physician who lived at the end of the twelfth century, and who had learned his art from a fairy who rose from a lake under the Black Mountains of Carmarthenshire, and whom he afterwards married, gave these directions : " Take a candle of mutton fat, mingled with seed of sea-holly, burn this candle as close as possible to the tooth, holding a basin of cold water beneath it. The worms (which are gnawing the tooth) will fall into the water to escape the heat of the candle." [8]

Exactly ! But neither the fairy nor her husband gave instructions as to what must be done when the tooth was still underground and the worms, presumably, underground with it.

Since nothing could be done to stop the burrowing, it seemed best to distract the mind of the sufferer. Would her lady's grace be minded to play with the white thrush that belonged to Princess Mary ? No, the white thrush would mean nothing at this moment. Should Jane the Fool come, with her cheeks round and shining and red as an apple under the new perwycke (periwig ?) bought for her by Princess Mary, — with her high crackling laughter, and her clothes that looked like the green herb paris, pointed and limp and created in the shade of a wood ? Or should Mr. Bingham, chaplain to my Lady Elizabeth's grace, be sent for to read her a story ? Her grace shook her head.

Lady Bryane, rocking her to and fro, pressing the Princess's round and aching cheek to her compassionate bosom, began to sing :

> " I had a little nut tree,
> Nothing would it bear
> But a silver nutmeg
> And a golden pear —
> And the King of Spain's daughter
> Came to visit me —
> And all because of
> My little nut tree.
> I skipped across the water —
> I skipped across the sea
> And all the birds of the air
> Could not catch me."

Once, years ago, Lady Bryane had sung this nursery song to another little child, Princess Mary — but her voice had died away with the words " Came to visit me ", for, standing behind the four-year-old Princess, almost as if it were cast by that innocent being, or as if it shared with her some secret, she had seen a black and terrible shadow, that of Juana of Castile, the King of Spain's daughter celebrated by the song, and the sister of the child's mother. Juana, married at seventeen to Philip of Burgundy, whom she loved passionately, and who was unfaithful to her, began to go insane at the age of twenty-three, then flamed into raging madness when she was twenty-six and that beloved traitor met his mysterious death. As she rushed like a comet across Spain to Granada, in her flight from those who would take the body of her husband from her, she seemed, now like a pillar of fire, now like a blackened ruin.

From time to time she would stop, and force her attendants to open the coffin, that she might see the dead body had not escaped from her. One of these days he would surely rise from his coffin, as she had often seen him rise from his bed after a long sleep. And this time he would not look at her coldly, but with a smile. But now no woman must approach him, for she would steal him from Juana. . . . And when, one night, she halted in the dark countryside with her train, only to find that she had taken the dead man, unwittingly, into a convent of nuns, she fled again, and then, in that night of storm, insisted on the coffin being opened, that she might see, by the wind-blown light of torches, that the dead man was still there.

It was this mad Queen whose visit to Henry VII was cele-brated in the nursery song. Lady Bryane, seeing that giant shadow evoked by the rhyme looming over her beloved charge, the four-year-old Mary, thought " She must never come again ". But now, when she looked at Mary, she saw the shadow ever standing behind her, waiting, as if it were listening for something — and that young face seemed changed as if the shadow were moulding her lineaments into its own likeness.

NOTES TO CHAPTER TEN

1 *Northumberland Household Books.*
2 Paul Friedmann, *Life of Anne Boleyn.*
3 *Ibid.*
4 These items are found in Queen Anne Boleyn's Accounts, paid after her death.
5 Chapuys to the Emperor, chapter 15, 1533.
6 Chapuys to the Emperor, December 16, 1533.
7 G. G. Coulton, *Social Life in Britain from the Conquest to the Reformation.*
8 *Ibid.*

H

Chapter Eleven

THE Lord Privy Seal smiled as he read Lady Bryane's letter ; for some minutes his heavy face bore that look of witty comprehension which was a part of his peculiar charm. He read the letter a second time, then put it aside. But it was not forgotten : for Lord Cromwell's encyclopedic memory was one of the causes of his rise to power. At this time, however, he had darker problems to deal with than the question of Princess Elizabeth's nightgowns, the interfering nature of Mr. Shelton, or even the thieving propensities of Sir John Nany, Knight of Little Egypt. The state apartments at Hampton Court rang with the furious roars of the King his master, or echoed with quiet tones which held a still greater menace.

The kingly will, the insensate obstinacy and vanity of Henry, encouraged by Cromwell's flatteries, had risen to a height, a violence, which astonished even that astute Minister.

"The lord Cromwell", wrote Bishop Gardiner in one of his letters, "had once put in the King's head to take upon him to have his will and pleasure regarded as a law ; and thereupon I was called for at Hampton Court. . . . 'Come on, my Lord of Winchester,' quoth he ; 'answer the King here, but speak plainly and directly, and shrink not, man. Is not that, quoth he, that pleaseth the King, a law ? Have not ye that in the civil laws ? . . .' I stood still and wondered in my mind to what conclusion this would tend. The King saw me musing, and with gentle earnestness said, 'Answer him whether it be so or no.' I could not answer the Lord Cromwell, but delivered my speech to the King, and told him that I had read of Kings that had their will recognised by law, but that the form of his reign to make the law his will was more sure and quiet ; and by this form of government ye be established, quoth I, and it is agreeable with the nature of your people. If ye begin a new policy, no man can tell."

The King turned his back, and left the matter.

Queen Elizabeth
The "Ermine" portrait at Hatfield

Anne Boleyn
National Portrait Gallery

Catherine Howard
National Portrait Gallery

King Henry VIII and his children (*from the engraving by William Rogers in the British Museum*)

But for some time after this conversation, his Highness would watch Gardiner when he thought that prelate was not looking — hastily averting his gaze when Gardiner turned towards him, for the King "though otherwise the most gentle and affable Prince in the world, could not abide to have any man stare in his face, or to fix his eye too steadily upon him when he talked with them.[1]

Henry had still an appearance of great magnificence and power. Though he was growing heavier, and the earth shook at his tread, he would yet indulge in contests with the bow — he who had drawn it more strongly than any man in England.

He was at this time much occupied with matters of faith. . . . There was, for instance, the question of Purgatory. In Latimer's *Remains* occurs this passage, with, in the margin, the King's remarks in his own handwriting : " The founding of Monasteries ", wrote Latimer, " argueth Purgatory to be ; so the pulling down of them argueth it not to be. What uncharitableness and cruelty seemeth it to destroy monasteries, if Purgatory be ! Now it seemeth not convenient " (for) " the Act of Parliament to preach one thing and the pulpit another clean contrary." To which the King added, in the margin, " Why then do you ? "

His Highness was much occupied also with family matters. " Squire Harry ", as Luther wrote a little later, " means to be God and to do as he pleases " (Juncke Heintze will Gott sein und thun was im gelüstet). After the death of Anne, a fresh will arose in him. " The King ", Chapuys told the Emperor, " has taken a fancy that the Princess Mary should consent to his statutes, or he would proceed against her."

Rebels against his regency under God must be crushed. Therefore, nothing would please him but that his daughter Mary should agree that she was born out of wedlock, that the marriage of her dead mother was incestuous and no marriage, and that everything on which her mother's life had been founded was a lie.

The new Queen, Jane, who was one of her dearest friends as well as her stepmother, weeping bitterly, tried to intervene, but the King, with a rude answer, put her entreaties aside.

Finding that his daughter returned evasive replies to his demands, the King sent the Duke of Norfolk, the Earl of Sussex, and other members of his Council, to Hunsdon, and they, seeing they could not overcome the Princess by argument, told her that " since she was so unnatural as to oppose the King's will so obstinately, they could scarcely believe she was his bastard ; and if she was *their* daughter they would beat her head against the wall till it was soft as a baked apple ".

The small red-headed creature, who had, in her mother's lifetime, defied the King and all the threats and wiles of her stepmother, was in a trap. The Princess's servants had been arrested and were held for questioning, and, at first, she was unable to communicate with Chapuys. There was no one near her to whom she could turn for advice, excepting warm-hearted, feather-witted Lady Bryane. And Lady Bryane could not advise her in such a matter as this.

But she had known Lord Cromwell since she was a little child ; for he had been Wolsey's factotum and had paid all the accounts of the royal nursery. He was one of her earliest memories, as a kind, good-natured, familiar being, under-standing of her difficulties ; and she turned to him in her terror and distress. But Cromwell knew his own life to be in danger because he had not succeeded in inducing Mary to obey the King, and in his fear for his own head and for hers, he threatened to desert her if she did not give way immediately to the demands of her " dear and benign father ". " To be plain with you," he wrote, " as God is my witness, I think you the most obstinate and obdurate woman, all things considered, that ever was ; and one that is so persevering, deserveth the extremity of mischief."

By this time she had succeeded in communicating with Chapuys, and he, knowing there was nothing else to be done, advised her to sign the documents sent her by Cromwell, " in order to save her life and that of her faithful servants, her honour and conscience being saved by protests which she would make apart, and by the obvious danger ".

She signed the papers, therefore, without reading them.

The document contained, following a humble plea for forgiveness, these clauses :

" I do recognise, accept, take, repute, and acknowledge, the King's highness to be the supreme head on earth, under Christ, of the Church of England, and do utterly refuse the Bishop of Rome's pretended authority, power, and jurisdiction, within this realm, hitherto usurped, according to the laws and statutes made on that behalf, and of all the King's true subjects humbly received . . . and after do utterly renounce all manner of remedy, interest, and advantage, which I may by any means claim by the Bishop of Rome's laws, process, jurisdiction, or sentence, at this present time, or in any wise hereafter. . . . Item, I do freely, frankly, and for the discharge of my duty towards God, the King's highness, and his laws, without any other respect, recognise and acknowledge that the marriage heretofore had between his Majesty and my mother, the late princess dowager, was by God's law and man's law incestuous and unlawful.

(signed) Mary." *

The shadow of Juana of Castile had come nearer. Mary was not changed outwardly, but her power of resistance against the King, even her will to combat his, had completely gone, while to all others it hardened. Bit by bit, the fearless girl, who had looked the usurper-Queen in the eyes, upholding her own and her mother's rights, changed, through the succeeding years, into the frantic dying creature whom history knows. She was separated now for ever from her mother, the being who had loved her most. Even death had not brought about so great a separation. She had betrayed her Church — perhaps the cruelties of her reign may be traced to this consciousness. But at the time, she felt nothing but joy, because of the reconciliation with her father. " Henry had been used to caress his daughter ", said Miss Strickland, " when domesticated with her ; there is no testimony that he ever used an angry word to her personally ; she loved him tenderly, and with natural self-deception attributed all the evil wrought against her mother and herself, to the machinations of Anne Boleyn. She thought if she were restored to the society of the King, instead of lingering

* Heame quotes all the articles — there are others besides those given here —as signed by Mary. Collier and Heylin affirm she did not sign the last two.

her life away in the nursery prison at Hunsdon, she should regain
the former interest in his heart."

In her gratitude, she wrote to Cromwell :

"Good Mr. Secretary, how much am I bound to you, which
have not only travailed, when I was almost drowned in folly,
to recover me before I sunk, and was utterly past recovery, and
so to present me to the face of grace and mercy ; but desisteth
not since, with your good and wholesome counsels, so to arm
me from my relapse, that I cannot, unless I were too wilful
and obstinate (whereof there is now no spark in me), fall again
into any danger.

"But leaving the recital of your goodness apart — which I
cannot recount — I answer the particulars of your credence
sent by my friend, Mr. Wriothesley. First, concerning the
princess" (Elizabeth) "(so I think I must call her yet, for I
would be loth to offend) ; I offered, at her entry to that name
and honour, to call her sister, but it was refused, unless I would
also add the other title unto it, which I refused then, not more
obstinately than I am sorry for it now, for that I did therein
offend my most gracious father and his just laws. And now you
think it meet, *I shall never call her by any other name than sister.*

"Touching the nomination of such women as I would have
about me, surely, Mr. Secretary, what men or women soever
the King's highness shall appoint to wait upon me, without
exception shall be to me right heartily welcome. Albeit, to
express my mind to you, I promise you, on my faith, Margaret
Baynton and Susanna Clarencieux * have, in every condition,
used themselves as faithfully, painfully, and diligently as ever
did women in such a case ; as sorry when I was not so con-
formable as became me, and as glad when I inclined to duty,
as could be devised. One other there is that was some time my
maid, whom for her virtue I love, and could be glad to have
in my company ; that is Mary Brown, and here be all that
I will recommend ; and yet my estimation of this shall be
measured at the King's highness my most merciful father's

* The daughter of the Clarencieux Herald ; she remained with Mary till
the latter's death.

pleasure and appointment, as reason is.

"For mine opinion, touching pilgrimages, purgatory, relics, and such like; I assure you I have none at all, but such as I shall receive from him who hath my whole heart in his keeping, that is, the King's most gracious highness, my most benign father, who shall imprint in the same, touching these matters and all other, what his inestimable virtue, high wisdom, and excellent learning shall think convenient and limit unto me. To whose presence, I pray God, I may come once ere I die, for every day is a year till I have a fruition of it.

"Beseeching you, good Mr. Secretary, to continue mine humble suit for the same, and for all other things whatsoever they be to repute my heart so firmly knit to his pleasure, that I can by no means vary from the direction and appointment of the same. And thus, most heartily, fare you well. From Hunsdon, this Friday, at ten o'clock of the night,

Your assured loving friend
Mary." [2]

There are several remarkable points about this letter, — her denial of any firm conviction about religious tenets, and her insistence on calling Elizabeth "princess". Her remarks about the latter show a certain bitter amusement. But she had the nobility, as Miss Strickland said, "to answer the agonised cry for forgiveness from the dying Anne Boleyn, by venturing a word in season for her forlorn little one". And in a letter written from Hunsdon on the 21st of July, she told the King: "My sister Elizabeth is in good health (thanks to our Lord), and such a child toward, as I doubt not, but your highness shall have cause to rejoice of in time coming (as knoweth Almighty God), who send your grace, with the queen my good mother, health, with the accomplishment of your desires".

The news of the King's full reconciliation with his eldest daughter reached her on the 17th of December 1536, when the Princess was summoned to Richmond Palace. . . . There, to quote from a contemporary report, she found " the King and the Quene standing in the chamber of presence by the fire. This worthy lady entered with all her train. So soon as she came within the chamber doore, she made low courtsey unto him ; in the midst of the chamber she did so againe, and when she came to them, she made them both low courtsey, and falling on her knees asked his blessing, who after he had given her his blessing, took her by the hand, and kiss't her, and the Quene also, both bidding her welcome. Then the King turning him to the Lords there in presence said : ' Some of you were desirous that I should put this jewel to death.' ' That were great pity,' quoth the Quene, ' to have lost your chiefest jewel of England.' . . . Then upon these words this good lady, knowing that when her father flattered most, mischief was like to ensue, her colour coming and going, at last in a swoon fell down amongst them. When that the King, being greatly perplexed . . . sought all possible means to recover her, and being come to herself, bid her be of good cheer, for nothing should goe against her, and after a perfect recovery, took her by the hand, and walked up and down with her ".[3]

Oh, the happiness of that Christmas and New Year spent in perfect reconciliation with her father ! The short winter days were spent in riding with her stepmother, in music, embroidery, and games of chance, — for Mary, like her father, was a gambler, and lost many angels at cards this Christmas-time, being obliged, one day, to " turn to Lady Carew for a loan when her pocket was empty ".[4] Presents were showered upon her, the King giving her the bordering for a dress of goldsmith's work. . . . This may have belonged to the Queen her mother, for she paid £4 : 3 : 4 to a goldsmith for lengthening the border, adding in her accounts (which she wrote with her own hand), " that the King's grace had given it to her ", noting, too, an additional sum paid to the goldsmith " for coming to Greenwich to take her orders ".[5] (The Court had left Richmond for Greenwich before Christmas Day.) . . . Lord Cromwell, delighted with the success of his peace-making, sent the Princess a " gift of sweet waters and fumes ". . . . She was sent a present, also, by the frightful Lady Rochford, now haunting the Queen as a lady-in-waiting.

In the months that followed that Christmas, the long-awaited rebellion against the King broke out. Known as the Pilgrimage

of Grace, it had come, at last, as the result of the proclamation
of the King's Supremacy, his power to bequeath the Crown
to whom he wished, the pronouncement that Mary was
illegitimate, and, above all, from the various miseries brought
about by the suppression of the monasteries, that " taught religion in the desert ways, gave doctoring and charity to the
poor, rest and refreshment to travellers, and succour to younger
sons, while the nunneries brought up daughters in virtue ".

The King told the deputies who came, at the beginning of
the rebellion, to lay their grievances before him, that he " marvelled that such ignorant dunces should talk of theological
subjects to him who something had been noted to be learned,
or should complain of his laws, as if, after twenty-eight years,
he did not know how to govern a kingdom, or should oppose
the suppression of the monasteries, as if it were not better to
relieve the head of the Church in his necessities, than to support
the sloth and wickedness of the monks ".

But in spite of this, the rebellion rose like a dust storm and
swept over the country. When it was over, the days were
made hideous by the sight of the King's vengeance, the nights
were filled by the sound of muffled footfalls, as the wives,
mothers, and daughters of the executed men crept out to cut
down the bodies and bury them in secrecy, or hide them in
ditches until such time as this could be done.

The two Princesses, on their way to Hampton Court to
attend the christening of their brother, late in that summer,
must have passed the frightful signs of vengeance, — the rotting
limbs and blackened heads boiled in pitch to preserve them, and
nailed to walls, bridges, posts — to every available monument
and object in the capital. Those signs were so many that the
authorities did not know where to dispose of them. " As the
gates of London are full of quarters not consumed," Lord
Chancellor Andelay told Cromwell on the 29th of March 1537,
" he has ordered the heads of . . . prisoners to be set upon
London Bridge, and at every gate, and the bodies to be buried."

During this time, far from their royal father's tempests of
rage and orgies of vengeance, the two disinherited Princesses
shared the Palace at Hunsdon.

The shadow of Lady Shelton seems to have vanished, and Mary ordered her own household, advised, no doubt, by the devoted Lady Bryane, who was still governess to the little Elizabeth.

Mary's old and faithful servants, who had been removed from her household, were now restored to her — Bess Cressy, and Randal Dod, Mary Fynche, " mother of the maids ", and Lucretia the Tumbler, and Thomas Crabtree, who was not only groom but messenger, going to fetch Dr. Nicholas, or taking presents of cucumbers and strawberries to the Queen and the Princess's other gossips.

In the green world of gardens and forests, Mary's quiet days began with an early morning reading of the daily service with her chaplain ; then followed lessons on the virginals from Mr. Paston, on the lute from Mr. van Wilder, of the King's privy chamber (for both these instruments the Princess had an extraordinary technical gift, inherited from her father). In the afternoons the Princess walked in the woods with her maids and visited the cottages of the poor. Or her numerous god-children would be brought to pay their respects to her, and to receive presents.

Elizabeth, now three and a half years old, would spend her days in listening to the more improving fairy-tales, recounted to her by Mr. Bingham, her chaplain, — who avoided, we imagine, such immoral works as " Margelone and the Fairy Melusine ", " Florice and Blanche ", and " Pyramus and Thisbe " — tales which had already been forbidden to Mary in her childhood.

Then there used to be rides to Banbury Cross on the knee of Lady Bryane or Elizabeth Candisshe, and sometimes (for Elizabeth could now run a short way without falling down) her sister Mary would change into a wolf and would chase her round a tree, and Elizabeth would hide in return, and run out from her hiding-place to catch Mary when she least expected it. . . . It is fun to catch another unawares. Neither Elizabeth nor Mary was frightened, one of the other. That time was yet to come . . . but now they were only playing at fear, and Elizabeth would run from Mary with a high bird-like scream, while Mary, pursuing her, laughed heartily, in a voice that was a little too deep for a woman.

It is difficult, now, to believe that the terrible figure that certain historians, and above all, Foxe, have shown us, had once been in reality a warm-hearted creature who felt pity and even tenderness for the little sister for whose sake she had been disinherited, — with a constant anxiety for the poor, and a charity for them that was as warm as love, — with a sense of fun, and a certain gaiety and charm. But such was the real Mary, before her disastrous love for Philip brought the darkening blight of her inheritance upon her, and before there came the final tragedy of the expected child she had nourished in her body, and that proved to be no child, but death.

We trace the peaceful life of Mary at Hunsdon, most clearly, in the household accounts kept by her with such care ; there, at this time, the most frequent of all entries are of sums paid for " Cucumbs " and for quails, sent by the Princess to Queen Jane.

For the time was coming when Princess Elizabeth would fulfil Lady Bryane's pious hope, and be " set abroad for the King's honour and hers ", at the christening of an heir to the throne. A child was about to be born to Queen Jane, and her state induced in her a longing for cucumbers and for quails. A dark cloud of quails, living and dead, descended upon Hampton Court, falling from the clouds, drifting from overseas. John Husee, factotum to Viscount Lisle, the King's illegitimate uncle, wrote frantic letters to Lord and Lady Lisle, demanding quails for the Queen's grace. He sent his lordship traps for quails by Anne and Agnes Woodruffe (whoever they may have been). He sent cages. The State Papers are full of eulogies and disparagements of these birds — they were too small or too big, they were not in their first youth, or they were delightfully plump and tender, they had arrived at the wrong time for supper, or had come at the right.

Lady Lisle was indefatigable in the matter, for she was a household goddess, according to the ideas of the time, and, too, she had two daughters by a previous marriage whom she wished placed as maids of honour.

But in spite of the pleasures and comforts of the Palace at Hampton Court, Queen Jane was, as Lady Lisle was told by her factotum, " horribly afraid of the Plague ", which, in the heat of the late summer and early autumn, crept over the island like a sea, and whose victims died " full of God's marks all over their bodies ".

" Our doctors ", said Thomas Dekker of a later plague, " gave that young Sickenesse . . . a fine gentleman-like name, the Spotted Feaver, as if it had been a beautiful faire-skin'd Sickenesse, and these spots the freckels . . . on the skin of it. But how many did this spotted Leopard set upon and teare in pieces." [6] " Art thou all spotted over ! They are God's riche Ermines ; to Inroabe thee like a King, and to set a Crowne of Glory on thy Head." [7] These plague-sores were of different colours. . . . " There were ", said William Bullein in his *Dialogue against the Feaver Pestilence*, " yelowe, redde, grene, and blacke. The first two are not so dangerous as the second two are. Yet, saith Rasis, in his book on the Pestilence, to Mansor the King, that the Carbuncle is deadlie and most perillous. And Amicen affirmeth the blacke to be incurable, specially when a feaver Pestilence doe reigne."

This plague, gaining force from the blackening limbs of the executed (nailed to gates, outposts, and walls of the city), carried from place to place by the stinking clothes the beggars had stolen from the bodies of the dead, spread through the suburbs (then the slums) and the " places of sin and stench ".

" In the first day of the sickness ", suggested William Bullein, [8] the patient must " bee kept from sleepe by talkynge, sprinkling of sweet waters, rubbing of the bodie, as nose, eares, — or soft pullyng of the eares . . . and have the chamber kept cleane before, and also perfumed fower times of the daie. Beware of stincke ; let the perfumes be made with Olibanum, Mastike, wood of Aloes, Benjamin, Storax, Laudanum, Cloves, Juniper, or such like ; and sprinckle all the chamber about with vinegar ; roses in the windowes, or greene braunches of Sallowe or of Quinces are good, sprinckled with Rose water and vinegar." . . .

Unhappily, the dwellers in the places of sin and stench did not follow these directions ; they did not pull ears softly, nor did they beware of stink, — and the plague spread.

But far from these places, Hampton Court was being prepared for the birth of the child who was to save England. All
precautions must be taken to ensure that no air should drift
from the limbs of the rebels and the bodies full of God's marks,
carrying death to the sheltered beings in the Palace.

King Henry's own Medycine for the Pestilence was kept in
readiness for the courtiers — (this was found among the manu-
scripts of Sir Hans Sloane) : ". . . Take an handfull of mary-
golds, a handful of sorel, and a handful of burnet, half a handful
of fetterfew, half a handful of rew, and a quantite of draggons
of the top or else of the roott, and weysshe them cleyne in
runnyng water, and let them seyth easily fro a potell on to a
quarte of liquor, and then sett yt back till it be almost cold,
and streyn yt theyn with a fyn cloth and drinck yt . . . and if
yt be takyn before that pimpulls do apere yt will hele the syke
person with God's Grace." [9]

At the same time, commanded by Dr. Sir William Buttes
and the other surgeons, " to have great store for the King ",
old Mr. George Aylsbury (who may, perhaps, have been
perfumer to the King), sent Lord Cromwell " the names of all
such infusions as I have made at this time of roses, after the
description " (recipe) " of Mesni, oil of roses, vinegar of roses,
rose-water, damask water, made chiefly of roses, dried roses.
. . . I would have made other if commanded, as conserve of
roses, syrup of roses, mel rosarum, julop of roses. . . . The
King hath sent for me to Hampton Court."

By this time, the two Princesses had arrived at the Palace ;
and on the 16th of September 1537, according to the rule by
which the Queen of England must be confined to her suite for
a month before the birth of her child, the Queen retired to her
rooms. On Friday, the 12th of October, the Vigil of St. Edward's
Day, after " a terrible travail ", she gave birth to the longed-for
heir.

Bishop Latimer, in his letter of congratulation to Cromwell
and the Privy Council, wrote, " here is no less joying and re-
joicing in these parts for the birth of our Prince, whom we
hungered for so long, than there was, I trow, by the neighbours

at the birth of John the Baptist. . . . God give us grace to yield
our thanks to our Lord God, the God of England, or rather an
English God, if we consider and pardon well His proceedings
against us from time to time."

"Incontinent after the birth," we read in the *State Papers*,
"the Te Deum was sung in St. Paul's and other Churches of the
city, and great fires made in every street, and banquetting and
triumphing cheer, with shooting of guns day and night, and
messengers were sent to all the estates and cities of the realm,
to whom were given great gifts."

The baptism of the saviour of England took place in the
chapel of Hampton Court at midnight on the Monday following
his birth.

And for this ceremony, Elizabeth was "set abroad for the
King's and Lord Cromwell's honour" — after a great deal of
fussing, weeping, and excitement, many exhortations, tugs, and
twitchings at hair, sleeves, and kirtle on the part of Lady Bryane.

The light of the full moon and of the great tapers shone
upon the silver font at the procession, which ended with the
Earl of Wiltshire, bearing a taper in silver : (for that cowardly
and sycophantic old man seems to have shown no reluctance to
attend the christening of Jane Seymour's child). Then came the
chrysome, "richly garnished, borne by the Lady Elizabeth, the
King's daughter (watched, we may well believe, by the anxious
eyes of Lady Bryane) — "the same lady for her tender age was
borne by Lord Beauchamp". Then came the Prince, under his
canopy. . . .

The ceremony over, the ladies Mary and Elizabeth were
served with spices, wafers, and wine, "then Lady Elizabeth
returned from the christening holding the hand of her sister
Mary, and with Lady Herbert of Troy bearing her train. And
the trumpets sounded."

The Sophoclean tragedy had ended in peace . . . the curse
of God was removed.

Or so it seemed.

But the child must be brought back in solemn state to the
Queen's chamber, to the sound of trumpets, and she, in order
to see the future King of England, must be removed from

her bed to a state pallet. The " most dear and entirely beloved son of our most dread and gracious lord Henry VIII " was placed in her arms.

But the Queen seemed tired : during the time of the christening, the King had remained with her : he talked loudly and unceasingly, in his joy. Next day, although it had seemed that she was recovering from the terrible hours of that protracted child-birth, she was so weak she could scarcely speak. The time of her triumph was not long. On Wednesday she was beyond caring for the things of this world. Yet still she lingered. It was not until the night that lay between the 24th and 25th of October that the last spark in that silent inexpressive creature was quenched for ever.

" Our mistress," wrote Wriothesley to Lord William Howard, then Ambassador to France, " through the fault of them that were about her, and suffered her to take great cold, and to eat things which the fantasye in her sickness called for, is departed to God."

She lay after her embalming, covered with a pall of cloth of gold whereon was set a cross, and candles burned night and day to light her sightless eyes. Her ladies knelt about the hearse, clad in black, with Princess Mary, her friend, to whom she had shown a great and loving kindness, as chief mourner. They watched the body of the dead Queen through the nights and days — the Princess contracting a raging toothache, due to cold, in that long watch. The ceremony of lying in state lasted until the 12th of November, when the funeral procession went its way from Hampton Court to Windsor, where the Queen was buried with great pomp.

These lines appeared on her tomb :

> Phoenix Jana jacet nato phoenice ; dolendum,
> Soecula phoenices nulla tulisse duos.

Her husband wrote this letter to the King of France :

" Il a semblé bon à la divine Providence, de mesler celle ma grande joie avec l'amaritude du trépas de celle qui m'avoit apporté ce bonheur.

" De la main de votre frère

Henry."

NOTES TO CHAPTER ELEVEN

[1] Puttenham, *Art of English Poesie.*
[2] Burnet, *History of the Reformation*, vol. ii. ; Hearne's *Sylloge* ; Strickland, *Mary I.* (Lives of the Queens of England.)
[3] Belvoir MSS., *Hist. MSS. Comm.* vol. i. Report XII. Appendix 4.
[4] Strickland, *Mary I.*
[5] *Ibid.*
[6] Thomas Dekker, *London Look Back.*
[7] Thomas Dekker, *The Black and White Rod.*
[8] William Bullein, *A Dialogue against the Feaver Pestilence.*
[9] Sir Henry Ellis, *Original Letters Illustrative of English History*, vol. ii.

Chapter Twelve

THE small disinherited Princess, after her public appearance at the christening of her half-brother, retired into private life, with Princess Mary. A person of no importance, she saw the whole of her life circling round the Prince for whom so much had been sacrificed, including the head of her own mother. . . . Even Lady Bryane seemed to belong now to the usurper. " My Lord Prince ", the chief governess told Lord Cromwell, " is in good health and merry. Would to God the King and your lordship had seen him last night, for his grace was marvellously pleasant disposed. The minstrels played, and his grace dawnsed and played so wantonly that he could not stand him still, and was as fol of prety toyes as ever I saw child in my lyfe." — And Lady Bryane went on to beg Lord Cromwell to show kindness to " my poor daughter Carew ", whose husband, formerly a companion of his Highness, had now, after a riotous life, been beheaded. " There is no house ", wrote Lady Bryane, " she can lye in, and I beg she may have Blecherynghe, which His Grace gave her without asking. . . . She has not been used to strait living, and it would grieve me in my old days to lose her."

Apparently the disgrace and execution of her son-in-law had made no breach between Lady Bryane and the King, who, with his strange royal generosity, gave her what she asked for.

Lady Bryane fussed and wept, or went into ecstasies over the new baby, clapping her hands at him, and bobbing up and down like a branch in the wind. There was, however, the usual trouble about clothes, and Cromwell's aid must be enlisted : " The best coat my lord prince's grace hath is tinsel, and that he shall have on at the time ; he hath never a good jewel for his cap ; howbeit I shall order all things for my lord's honour the best I can, so as I trust the King's grace shall be contented withal ; and also master vice-chamberlain and master cofferer I am sure will do the best diligence that lieth in them in all causes."

Then comes a brighter note : " My lord, I thank Jesu, my lord prince's grace is in good health and merry, and his grace hath four teeth ; three full out, and the fourth appeareth. And thus fare you well, my good lord " [1]

Elizabeth, in her nursery in another Palace, had a rival ; but she was not neglected   " She was not permitted ", wrote the Reverend Joseph Stevenson, editor of the *Calendar of State Papers in the reign of Elizabeth*, " to neglect such small household duties as she could perform. When she was six years old, she presented to her brother Prince Edward a shirt of cambric as a New Year's gift, and a year later, at the same festival, the gift was needle-work of her making   She sewed, and she did her lessons, — learning the alphabet from a " delicate little horn-book of silver filagree ". " In shape ", wrote Mr. Walter de la Mare in *Come Hither*, " they " (horn-books) " resembled a small oblong hand-glass, with a hole through the handle ; a piece of string was passed through the hole, and the horn-book was tied round the owner's waist. Fixed and fitted to one side of it was an oblong strip of parchment, card, or paper, containing the criss-cross row (the Alphabet with a cross before A) a few dia-graphs, Ah, ba, and so on, ' In the name of the Father ' and the Lord's prayer."

But there were other matters beyond sewing a seam, and deciphering the alphabet, that Elizabeth learned at this time.

From now, until she was ten years old, when we hear of her being banished from Court for having offended her father (how, we know not : perhaps she had asked what had been the fates of her mother, and of that later stepmother who had also, at that time, been thrust into a blood-stained grave) — we know but little of Elizabeth. No echo of her voice comes to us : nor do we see her face. Yet in the intervening years of silence be-tween those ages of childhood, she must have learned much. It is dangerous to give your heart into another's keeping — or your thoughts. Henry thought he had the right to " make a window into the hearts of all men " : but there should be no window into the heart of Elizabeth. This was the earliest lesson learned by the future Queen of England : to speak your thoughts means danger. To love means danger. What is high today is low tomorrow — so low that it is part of the dust.

People came and went at the Court of Henry like the tall grave shadows of evening, going to meet the universal darkness, — or like happy little summer shadows flying over the grass. These shadows changed according to the light of the sun or the will of the King.

Two years had passed since the death of Jane Seymour, and the King decided to marry again. But though his grace the Prince was marvellously pleasant disposed, and danced and played, his royal father was restless in another fashion, breeding a black and destructive rage. The hidden plague that had destroyed all his male children by Catherine, invaded his whole body, slow drop by drop. "The King", the French Ambassador told Montmorency, "has stopped one of the fistulas of his legs, and for ten or twelve days the humours which had no outlet were like to have stopped his breath, so that he was sometimes without speaking, black in the face, and in great danger."

At that time, those who surrounded the King were in constant peril, threatened, often, by a hidden menace whose face was unknown to them, whose speech was not understood.

"As for my lord Privy Seal" (Cromwell), wrote George Paulet in 1538, well before the King's fourth marriage, "I would not be in his case for all that he hath, for the King beknaveth him twice a week, and sometimes knocketh him over the pate ; and yet when he hath been well pounded about the head, and shaken up as it were a dog, he will come out into the great chamber, shaking of the bush " (hair) " with as merry a countenance as though he might rule all the roast."

Each step taken, each word uttered, must be guarded. And the day came when the low-born Cromwell was a little tired. Fatigue caused in him a moment's carelessness. He had been too used to flattering, to saying what he thought would please. Now, occupied with finding a new bride for the King, he told his master that Anne, Princess of Cleves, sister to the reigning Duke, excelled the Duchess of Milan " as the golden sun excelleth the sylvern moon ".

The unfortunate sun came, and was found lacking in warmth. The sun did not shine.

The future Queen of England was met, a mile from Calais, by the Lord High Admiral of England, the Earl of Southampton, dressed in purple velvet and cloth of gold, tied with great aglets and trefoils of gold, and wearing round his neck the insignia of his office, a gold whistle. With him were gentlemen in blue velvet and crimson satin : while the sailors on the ship waiting to escort their King's bride were clothed in satin of Bruges.

The Princess was welcomed by the royal salute of guns. — Then, owing to the weather, she was delayed at Calais until the 27th of December, on which day she arrived at Rochester.

On New Year's Eve, the King, who had succeeded in persuading himself that he had fallen in love with the Princess's portrait, informed Cromwell (according to Hall's *Chronicle*) that he " intended to visit her privately on the morrow, to nourish love ".

In this romantic mood he, with eight gentlemen of his privy chamber, dressed, like their master, in marble-colour, rode to Rochester, and the King entered the room where his bride was sitting.

One look was enough. The King, deeply shocked at the duplicity of his advisers, strove, at this first meeting, to disguise his feelings from his bride. He "welcomed her with gracious words ", said Hall, " and gently took her up and kissed her ". But the moment he could disengage himself from the conversation — which must be translated backwards and forwards, as the bride could speak no language known to the King — he left her presence, and sent for the Admiral.

" How like you this woman ? " he enquired. " Do you think her so personable, fair, and beautiful, as report hath been made to me ? I pray you tell me true."

The Admiral, a man of tact, replied, " I take her not for *fair*, but to be of a *brown* complexion."

" Alas ! " said the King. " Whom shall man trust ? I promise you, I see no such thing as hath been shown me of her by picture or report. I am ashamed that men should praise her as they have done, and I love her not."

At those words a chill must have crept through the blood of Cromwell.

His grace could not bring himself to present in person the

partlet and "muffly furred" of rich sables that he had bought as a New Year's gift for his bride, but sent these, with a cold message, by Sir Anthony Browne, his Master of the Horse.

Meanwhile, an altercation had broken out between the Lord High Admiral, who had brought the bride from Calais, and Cromwell, who was anxious to shift the blame. Why, enquired Cromwell furiously, could he not have kept the lady at Calais? He had *seen* her! Then why on earth had he brought her to England?

But the Admiral was not prepared to shoulder the blame. He answered that "he was not invested with any such authority. His commission was to bring her to England, and he had obeyed his orders." To this, Cromwell replied that the Admiral " had spoken in his letters of the lady's beauty in terms of commendation, which had misled his highness and the Council ".

The Admiral countered by saying that "as the Princess was generally reported for a beauty, he had only repeated the ideas of others, for which no one ought reasonably to blame him, especially as he supposed she would be his Queen".

The conversation was interrupted at this point by a peremptory message from the King, giving orders that by some means or another he must be disentangled from the engagement.

But the lady was here, and must be disposed of somehow. Before her arrival, orders had gone forth that all loyal subjects who were able to do so, were to muster at Greenwich to witness the happiness of their King, and to welcome his bride. The loyal subjects had obeyed. The Princess was, consequently, escorted to Greenwich in great state, and the enormous waiting crowd was rewarded by a touching scene. "As soon", said Hall, "as she" (the Princess) "and the King, had alighted from their horses, in the inner Court, the King lovingly embraced her, and bade her welcome to her own, then led her by the left arm through the hall, which was furnished below the hearth with the King's guard, and above the hearth with fifty pensioners with their battle-axes, and so brought her up to her privy chamber."

He then withdrew immediately to his own chamber, and, sending for Cromwell, ordered him to call a Council to discuss what could be done to stop the marriage. . . . They must enquire, for instance, whether there had not been a pre-contract between the Princess and the Marquis of Lorraine.

But next morning (Sunday) Cromwell, entering the King's room by the private way,[2] informed the King that there was no hope of establishing the existence of a pre-contract. The lords who had accompanied the Princess to England had even gone so far as to offer themselves as hostages, so certain were they of this. . . . On which the King exclaimed : " I am not well handled. If it were not that she is come so far into my realm, and the great preparation that my states and people have made for her, and for fear of making a ruffle in the world and of driving her brother into the hands of the Emperor and the French King, who are now together, I would not marry her."

And he insisted again that the existence of a pre-contract *must* be found. The Princess must make a solemn declaration, one way or the other. The Minister was obliged to tell his master that strict enquiries had been made, and no pre-contract existed. . . . Whereupon he said, not for the first time, " Is there none other remedy but that I must needs against my will put my neck into the yoke ? "

Cromwell could think of nothing better to say than that " he was sorry his Grace was not better pleased ". He then withdrew, leaving his Grace in " a study of pensiveness " — to quote his own courtier-like description of his master's state.

In that " study " his Grace remained until the day of the wedding, when, with dragging footsteps, he went to the altar, and placed upon his bride's finger a ring inscribed with the words " God send me well to kepe ".

It was a marriage in name only.

The Queen could do nothing right. Her manners were outlandish, she had " displeasant airs ", and the wife of the Master of the Horse told her husband that " she saw in the queen such fashions, and manner of bringing up so gross, that she thought the King would never love her ". . . . She could not sing : she took no interest in music — and Henry was a superb musician. The King complained to Cromwell that she was silent and glum-looking, and threatened that if this continued, he would divorce her.

A few days afterwards he noticed that now, far from looking glum, she had adopted a winning manner, and smiled unweariedly upon him !

This was too much ! It was obvious to the King that Cromwell must have repeated every word of his complaint. Was there *no one* whom he could trust ? . . . He began to meditate upon his Minister's conduct.

The marriage had been brought about by Cromwell — oh yes, it had ! Cromwell had thought nothing of his master's personal happiness — he had not considered it !

Now the Minister, having made one slip, felt his foothold insecure. He had lost his sense of certainty. And now another mistake was to be made through him.

Cromwell had never thought it possible that the King of France and the Emperor should become real allies, and Henry, misled by his Minister, thought it would be possible to tempt Francis away from his partner — to instil doubts in him. . . . It must be suggested to the French King that the Emperor aspired to make all Christendom into an empire — under his rule ! But if the French King would only join the league being formed between the King of England and his brother-in-law the Duke of Cleves, the Elector of Saxony, the Landgrave, and other Princes of the Empire, they would, as Henry told the Duke of Norfolk,[3] " have the Emperor in such a pitfall that percase it might be their chance to take him prisoner at their pleasure, his being so environed with them, and having no way to start ".

The proposal was based on a total misapprehension ; it failed therefore, — and the failure was Cromwell's fault.

But worse was to come. The German Princess saw the danger of an open quarrel with the Emperor, and the Emperor induced them to believe that he would allow a mediation on their behalf, made by the Duke of Cleves.

Henry found himself alone, though he had a wife — the wife whom he had married in order to secure these allies.

Yet in April, a few days after the meeting of Parliament,

his Majesty bestowed upon his Minister the title of Earl of Essex
— as a mark of his approbation.

"To the eyes of the world," said Froude, "' the hammer of
the monks' remained absolute as ever. No cloud, as yet, was
visible in the clear sky of his prosperity : when the moment
came, he fell suddenly, as if struck by lightning, on the very
height and pinnacle of his power."

Did Cromwell feel any warning, in nerves or mind ? The
King was in a thoughtful state, asking himself why he was
unable to love his bride. "I have done as much to move the
consent of my heart and mind as ever man did," he told his
Minister, "but without success." On another occasion, "I
think before God", he exclaimed, "she has never been my
lawful wife." He said, too, that "he was in a manner weary
of his life ".

Wriothesley, going to Cromwell's house on his usual business,
"found the minister alone in a gallery, leaning against a
window ". He told Cromwell that some way must be found
by which to disentangle the King from his marriage. But
Cromwell seemed despondent.

Next day, Wriothesley reverted again to the matter : "For
God's sake, devise for the relief of the King, for if he remain in
this grief and trouble, we shall all one day smart for it. If his
grace be quiet we shall all have our parts with him."[4]

Cromwell was in despair. The first divorce had alienated
the Catholics, this would alienate the Lutherans. What would
the Pope say ? And the Emperor ? — Think of the scandal —
as if there had not been enough already ! . . . And then there
was the question of the wool trade, on which the finances of the
country largely depended. There were the merchants, the wool-
growers, to be thought of.[5] All these, " in the connection with
the house of Cleves, saw a fresh cause of quarrel with the
Emperor, and the ruin of the trade with Flanders ". — In the
hope of gaining allies, the woman had been brought here. And
now the allies had vanished, but the woman was left, and the
King wished to divorce her, and everything would have been
of no avail.

Cromwell began to mistrust his own judgment. "The

triumph of his enemies ", said Froude, " stared him in the face ",
yet he now spoke rashly, perhaps from some kind of defiant
despair, despising those enemies. And he had many. Not for
nothing had he been, for years, the final court of appeal for the
whole country, arbitrating between husbands and wives, sons
and parents, between neighbours and between litigants of all sorts.

The Duke of Norfolk had not forgotten that Cromwell
had listened to the termagant Duchess's half-mad diatribes
against him. The Lord High Admiral had not forgotten that
attempt to shift the blame of the arrival of the future Queen.

On the 10th of June Cromwell attended the morning sitting
of the House of Lords ; and, in the afternoon, the Privy Council.
At three o'clock the Duke of Norfolk, without warning, rose
from the table. " My Lord of Essex," he said, " I arrest you
of High Treason.[6] Then came the witnesses, who swore they
had heard him say " that if the King and all his realm would
turn and vary from his opinions " (on the subject of the Reformation), " he would fight in the field in his own person, with his
sword in his hand, against the King and all others, adding that
if he lived a year or two he trusted to bring things to that frame
that it should not lie in the King's power to resist or let it ".[7]

Marillac gave the Constable of France the following account
of the arrest (23rd June 1540) : [8] " The arrest took place in the
Council Chamber at the Palace at Westminster. The Lieutenant
of the Tower entered with the King's commands to take him
prisoner. In a burst of passion he clutched his cap and flung it
on the ground. ' This, then,' he said to the Duke of Norfolk
and the rest of the Council assembled there, ' is my guerdon
for the service that I have done. On your consciences, I ask
you, am I a traitor ? I may have offended, but never with my
will. Such faults as I have committed deserve grace and pardon ;
but if the King my master believes so ill of me, let him make
quick work and not leave me to languish in prison.' "

Part of the Council exclaimed that he was a traitor, part
that he should be judged by the bloody laws that he had himself
made ; words idly spoken he had twisted into treason ; the
measure which he had dealt to others should now be meted out
to him.

The Duke of Norfolk, after reproaching him for his many villainies, tore the Order of St. George from his neck. The Admiral, to show that he was as much his enemy in adversity as, in prosperity, he had pretended to be his friend, stripped off the Garter. He was then led down into a barge which opened on the river, and was rowed to the Tower.

The charges against him included not only that of high treason, but accepting bribes, and causing heretics to be set at liberty.

Now he, a prisoner in the Tower, crying for " Mercy — mercy " — and receiving it as little as those whom he had helped to bring to their deaths (Anne Boleyn, the martyrs, and the opposers of the King's will) — found only one friend in his misery. Cranmer, with extraordinary courage — all the greater because he was, by nature, timid —, wrote this letter to the King :

" I heard yesterday in your Grace's council, that the Earl of Essex is a traitor ; yet who cannot be sorrowful and amazed that he should be a traitor against your Majesty — he whose surety was only by your Majesty — he who loved your Majesty — as I thought, no less than God — he who studied always to set forward whatsoever was your Majesty's will and pleasure — he that cared for no man's displeasure to serve your Majesty — he that was such a servant, in my judgment, in wisdom, diligence, faithfulness and experience as no prince in this realm ever had — he that was so vigilant to preserve your Majesty from all treasons, that few could so secretly be conceived but he detected the same in the beginning ! — I loved him as my friend, for so I took him to be ; but I chiefly loved him for the love which I thought I saw him bear ever towards your Grace, singularly above all others. But now, if he be a traitor, I am sorry that ever I loved or trusted him ; and yet I am very glad that his treason is discovered in time ; but yet, again, I am very sorrowful ; for who shall your Grace trust, hereafter, if you may not trust him ? Alas ! I lament your Grace's chance herein. I wot not whom your Grace may trust." [9]

But the letter was of no avail ; and in a short time, Cromwell having signed the documents declaring that the King's new marriage had never been consummated, his use was over ; and his head was hacked from his body, with many strokes, by " a beggarly fellow with a ragged knife ".

Anne of Cleves, rather to the King's surprise, accepted the divorce, and a position as the King's adopted sister, with a large allowance, without any visible regret.

She was, said Hollingshed, " a lady of right commendable regard, courteous, gentle, a good housekeeper, and very bountiful to her servants ".

These loved her dearly. She was also a placid-natured woman, and now that the King was released from the marriage, he became on excellent terms with her. She was devoted to his daughters, and they returned her affection.

The ex-Queen's amiable attitude to her ex-husband may have surprised the Court and the diplomats. But they were more than surprised — they were astonished — at the sudden splendour of her attire. The divorce over, she appeared in a new dress every day, and each dress was " more wonderful than the last ".[10]

NOTES TO CHAPTER TWELVE

[1] E. Green, *Letters of Royal and Illustrious Ladies*, vol. iii.
[2] Strickland, *Anne of Cleves*. (Lives of the Queens of England.)
[3] Henry Froude, *Henry VIII*.
[4] Strype, *Memorials*, vol. ii. ; Froude, *Henry VIII*.
[5] Froude, *Henry VIII*.
[6] *Ibid*.
[7] *Ibid*.
[8] *Ibid*.
[9] Cranmer to the King, quoted by Lord Herbert of Cherbury ; *Life of King Henry VIII*.
[10] Dispatches of Marillac.

Chapter Thirteen

IT is strange how ordinary a ghost can seem! When we look upon it for the first time, its occupation is probably a small one, so as to make it seem as if it were living.

Perhaps it would crouch outside a door, listening to the voices in the room beyond, waiting for the door to be opened. Or, standing in a ray of sunlight by a window, it would give, with a quick secret movement, a little ruby ring to one whose face could not be seen, because it was in shadow. Or, looking in a mirror, it would pin a cheap artificial flower — a silk pansy — over the place where its heart should have been.

Anne Boleyn was dead, but out of her grave, a horrible but infinitely pitiable little ghost, a travesty of her sin (real or imagined), crept to strike down the King who had been her husband.

Now in the rooms which the dead Queen had inhabited, fresh footsteps sounded. . . . Then, as you turned the corner of a gallery, a small figure would be seen coming towards you — the figure of a very young girl — or of an evil child, a child of about thirteen, with a terrible adult knowledge. For she hardly looked more than the age at which she had begun her somnambulistic walk to the scaffold.

About midsummer, just before the King's divorce from Anne of Cleves, rumour spread about the Court that the King had fallen in love again, and this time with " a very little girl " ; Katherine Howard, stepdaughter of the old Duchess of Norfolk (in whose house she, as a motherless child, had been brought up), and cousin german to Anne Boleyn.

The King was often seen going, in his barge, to visit her, in the daytime, and sometimes at night.

The Bishop of Winchester provided feasting for them at his palace.

The " very little girl " in her new finery — it was the first time in her life she had been given decent clothes — seemed

ready to dance with happiness. No more buffetings and beatings
. . . the old Duchess would not dare ! For if she did, Katherine
would tell the King.

The monarch fell more and more deeply in love with the
youth, the modesty, the innocence of this cousin of his late wife.

She was an outwardly charming young creature, little and
gay as a golden mote of light — and as quickly gone. But
though this girl on whose golden eyelashes the sun seemed to
rest, was in her earliest youth, that youth had its secrets.

One day as she — then nineteen years old at the utmost —
stood on the threshold of Queenship, a letter reached her. It
contained these words :

" I beseech you to save some room for me which you shall
think fit yourself, for the nearer I am to you, the gladder I
would be. . . . I beseech you not to be forgetful of my request,
for if you do not help me, I am not like to have worldly joys.
Desiring you if you can, to let me have some answer of this
for the satisfying of my mind, for I know the Queen of England
will not forget her secretary

your humble servant
with heart unfeigned
Jone Bulmer."

Reading these words, the future Queen of England turned a
greenish white.

There had been days, above all, there had been nights, when
she was a child of thirteen and fourteen, a young girl of fifteen
and sixteen, — whose secrets were known to her grandmother's
waiting-women. They knew, for they had witnessed everything.

How many people knew those secrets ? Katherine tried to
remember, and a sick terror invaded her as she thought of their
number. Oh, if only those days and nights could be obliterated
from the living memory — or if the living people who knew
all could be dead.

Whether that letter was, or was not, a veiled threat, is not
known. But Katherine had now only two alternatives. Either
she must become Queen, menaced, night and day, by the fear

that her terrible secret would be disclosed, — or she must reveal
the secret that lay behind the cautious words of that letter, and
renounce all hope of becoming Queen. She chose the former
course, and gave Joan Bulmer a place about her person.

This woman, who had been her bedfellow in the house of
the Duchess, was also " entertained by " (*i.e.* was the mistress
of) Francis Dereham. She was now married to a young man
named Bulmer. Katherine yielded now to her demands, for
indeed she had no real choice in the matter. There was no one
to whom she could turn. She had no friends, and the old
Duchess of Norfolk, determined she should be Queen, had
assured the King of her fitness, her eminent suitability to be
his wife.

That terrible old woman had so neglected her grandchild
that to buy any little piece of finery she must borrow money
from Francis Dereham, a distant kinsman who lived in the
Duchess's house. In this way she procured a silk pansy, some
little pieces of velvet, a cap with velvet knots. . . .

She thought, now, of those rags of finery, — and of the
payment of them, made to Dereham in those nights and days
of her late childhood, and remembering this, she was filled with
hatred, of Dereham, of her grandmother, of everyone concerned.

The marriage that made Katherine Queen of England was
solemnised in profound secrecy, a few hours after the divorce
of the Princess of Cleves ; on the 8th of August the new Queen
took up her residence at Hampton Court, and was prayed for,
as Queen, in the churches.

The King's infatuation for his new wife seemed greater,
according to the French Ambassador, than his love had been
for any other woman. The domestic happiness of his family
seemed assured, the new Queen played with, and spoiled, the
little stepdaughter who was also her cousin, and, after a childish
quarrel with Mary, made friends with her and welcomed her
at Court.

The young Queen made a few changes in the royal household, taking into her service certain persons who had been
about her in her childhood and earliest girlhood ; Katherine
Tylney, who had been one of the Duchess's waiting-women —

and Francis Dereham, who became her secretary. . . . One
Henry Manox, only too well known to the Queen, entered
the household as a musician. Joan Bulmer was one of her bed-
chamber women. And the frightful Lady Rochford, a lady-in-
waiting, became one of her young mistress's most intimate
companions.

At first, the life at the Court was gay ; then, after a few
months, the King's illness returned, taking the form, at first,
of a tertian fever. . . . The French Ambassador told Montmorency " the King's life was really thought to be in danger,
not from the fever but from the leg, which often troubles him
because he is very stout and marvellously excessive in eating
and drinking, so that people say . . . he is often different in
the morning than [sic] he is after dinner. . . . He has a *mal
d'esprit*, hearing that his subjects murmured at the changes imposed upon them and at their ill-treatment for religious opinions ;
and having conceived a sinister opinion of some of his chief
men during illness, he said he had an unhappy people to govern,
whom he would shortly make so poor that they would not have
the boldness nor the power to oppose him ; and that most of his
Privy Council, under pretence of obeying him, were only tem-
porising for their profit : but he knew the good servants from
the flatterers, and if God lent him health, he would take care
that their projects should not succeed. . . . Sometimes he even
reproached " (his Ministers) " with Cromwell's death, saying
that upon light pretexts, by false accusations, they had made
him put to death the most faithful servant he ever had ". . . .
For now Cromwell had gone, not even the uncombatable kingly
will could restore that much-needed faithfulness to life.

The King said " it was time to arise from his sick-bed, for
the ramparts of Dover, Portsmouth, and elsewhere " (continued
the Ambassador) " are clean fallen down, and the King is so
angered that he will go in person and direct how they are to
be rebuilt ".

Shrovetide, owing to the King's mood, was passed in a
sinister silence. . . . There was no music, in spite of the King's
passion for it . . . there were few visitors, and the business of
these was asked, and they were often sent back, as if something

within the Palace must be kept hidden.

In that strange silence it seemed, almost, as if all were waiting for the tread of Doom in the long passages, the empty state apartments. . . . But when that step was heard, it was not a giant sound, like that of a being of stone, endowed suddenly, after long ages, with a terrible life : it was a little, light step, like that of Anne Boleyn. . . .

The King recovered, slowly, and began, that summer — (he had been married for rather less than a year) — a royal progress to York with his new Queen. The preparations for the tour were of such magnificence that Marillac told the French King " they seem to betoken some extraordinary triumph ".

The royal procession halted at various stages on the journey, and the days and nights, during those halts, were one round of pleasures and sports. At Hatfield, for instance (according to the *State Papers*), " where there are ponds and marshes, with boats on the water and bows on land, were slain in one day 200 stags and does, and next day, two miles off, was scarcely less slaughter. In the King's presence was taken in the water a great quantity of young swans, two boats full of river birds, and as much of great pikes and other fish ; so that with the same enclosure they took at one time both flesh and fish. Henry requested Marillac to tell the French King of this, and afterwards, when the Ambassador was supping with him in his tent, King Henry pointed at two or three hundred stags, as near the company as if they had been domesticated cattle, or those enclosed in parks."

One day in August, possibly during the stay at Hatfield, one of the Queen's maids, Margryt Morton, saw her mistress looking out of the window. Partly from idle curiosity, and partly from malice — for she hated the Queen, who had ordered her not to enter the royal bedroom unless she was called — Margryt looked to see what the Queen was watching. She was " looking out of the window on Mr. Culpepper " — her cousin, and one of the King's most intimate companions.

The waiting, watching maid, seeing that look, came to a certain conclusion.

A little later, when the Court had reached Lincoln, Thomas Culpepper received a strange letter :

" Master Culpepper, I heartily recommend me unto you, praying you to send me word how you do. I heard you were sick, and never longed so much for anything as to see you. It makes my heart die to think I cannot always be in your company."

Then, after a few words about horses, and a manservant who was to be employed, the letter ends —

" Yours as long as lyffe endures

Katheryn."

The maids were whispering among themselves. . . . It was said that while the Court was at Lincoln, on the Progress, the King, one night, had found the Queen's door locked ; and that it was some little time before it was undone and he was admitted. Then, one night, the Queen had left her room, very late, and had gone, unaccompanied, to the room of Lady Rochford, " which was up a little stair ".

Katheryn Tylney, one of the Queen's maids (who had been among her companions in the Duchess of Norfolk's house), and Margryt her fellow were already in bed. But Margryt rose to follow her. She was not admitted to the room, but waited upon the stair. At two o'clock in the morning Katheryn was awakened by Margryt returning to bed. " Christ," she exclaimed, " is not the Queen returned yet ? " " Even now," replied Margryt.

The Queen's maids by now spied on her every action. For " when they were at Pontefract ", said Margryt Morton, in her evidence, " the Queen had angry words with Mrs. Lyffkyn " (mother of the Chamberers) " and herself, and forbade their attendance in her bedchamber ".

She had made two mortal enemies.

. . . . . .

The strange comings and goings continued.

One night the Watch, appearing with a torch at the back door of the royal apartments, saw the muffled figures of two women, obviously waiting for someone. They disappeared silently, and the Watch locked the door. But presently two men appeared, and picking the lock, entered. One of those men was Culpepper.

K

Mysterious messages, not to be understood by the bearer, were sent by the Queen to Lady Rochford (Katheryn Tylney being the messenger) — and equally strange messages were sent in reply. . . . At Hampton Court the maid was " bade to go to my Lady Rochford and ask when she should have the thing she promised her ; and she (Lady Rochford) answered that she sat up for it, and she would the next day bring her word herself. A like message and answer was conveyed to, and from, my lord of Suffolk."

As Miss Strickland noted, the Duke of Suffolk had been the husband of the King's sister. It is hardly likely that he could have been aiding the Queen in her nefarious love-plots. It is therefore probable that the secret related to money, or the private purchase of jewels, which the Queen wished " to procure in an underground way ". "Katherine," Miss Strickland continues, " like all persons who have been early initiated into the dark mysteries of sin, had evidently acquired a systematic habit of concealment, even with regard to those trifling actions which, when openly performed, would never excite suspicion."

The royal tour was at an end, and the King and Queen returned to Hampton Court on the 30th of October, the day before the Festival of All Souls. Next day, a thanksgiving was to be made in the churches to Almighty God for the happiness bestowed on His Regent on earth by the gift of so virtuous and loving a wife.

But as the King returned from Mass and the Thanksgiving, he found Archbishop Cranmer waiting for him. The Archbishop was deathly pale, and spoke in a low voice. He placed in the King's hands a paper, asking him to read it when he should be alone.

That paper told part of the story of Katherine's corrupted childhood and early youth. During the royal tour, John Lassels, brother of one of the vile women who, in the Duchess of Norfolk's household at Lambeth, had watched the downfall of this neglected and friendless child, had come to the Archbishop and old him what Mary Lassels had seen.

The haunted King, met at last, at the end of a long passage, by the waiting ghost, swore that the Queen was calumniated, and that this was a plot against her. His agony was frightful to witness. — He persisted in believing nothing against her.

But the story must be investigated, and until this was done, the Queen must know nothing. Nor must any rumour reach the Court, lest her reputation should be touched.

But the Court knew that something strange was happening. Why was there a pretence that the King was hunting, in order to explain his absence from the Palace ? Why had the Council, including the Duke of Norfolk (who was in quarantine because one of his servants had died of the plague), been summoned in the middle of the night ? The King had left Hampton Court without seeing the Queen, — without sending her a message. What did that mean ?

Then, later in the day, the Council appeared, and were shown into the Queen's presence.

Then the Queen's voice was heard, raised to a scream. And after the Council left her, she fell into fits of shrieking, of so frightful a nature that it was supposed, through the night, that she would either die or go mad.

The Court knew, now, that the Council had brought charges against her, and that she had denied them with frenzy.

Next morning the Archbishop went to her, bearing a message from the King, promising her that if she would acknowledge her guilt, " the King had determined to extend to her his most gracious mercy ".

For at this time only the sins of her early youth were known ; her behaviour — guilty or only foolish — after her marriage had not yet been divulged.

Cranmer, filled with pity for her, wrote to the King :

" I found her in such lamentation and heaviness as I never saw no creature, so that it would have pitied any man's heart in the world to have looked upon ; and in that vehement rage " (agony) " she continued, as they informed me which be about her, from my departure until my return again, and then I found her, as I do suppose, far entered towards a frenzy " (madness) " which I feared before my departure from her at my first being with her. Surely if your grace's comfort had not come in

time, she could have continued no long time in that condition
without a frenzy, which, nevertheless, I do much suspect to
fall hereafter. . . .

" After I had declared your grace's mercy with her, she held
up her hands, and gave most humble thanks with your majesty,
who had shewed her more grace and mercy than she herself
thought meet to sue for, or could have hoped for. Then, for
a time, she became more temperate and moderate, saving that
she still sobbed and wept ; but after a little pausing, she suddenly fell into a new rage, much worse than before. Now I do
use her thus — when I do see her in any such extreme braid "
(paroxysms) " I do travail with her to know the cause, and then,
as much as I can, I do labour to bate away, or at least to mitigate,
the cause. . . .

" I told her there was some new fantasy come into her
head, which I desired her to open unto me ; and after a certain
time, when she had recovered herself that she might speak, she
cried and said :

" ' Alas, my lord, that I am alive — the fear of death did
not grieve me so much before as doth now the remembrance
of the King's goodness — for when I remember how gracious
and loving a prince I had, I cannot but sorrow. . . .'

" And for all I could say to her, she continued in a great
pang a long while. After that, she began something to remit
her rage, and come to herself ; she was metely " (fairly) " well
until night, and I had good communication with her, and, as
I thought, brought her into a great quietness. Nevertheless,
at night, at about six o'clock, she fell into another pang, but not
so outrageous as the first ; and that was (as she shewed me)
because of remembrance that at that time in the evening, Master
Heneage was wont to bring her news of your Grace."

The wretched creature was weeping because of what she
had done to the only being who had ever shown her kindness
. . . Henry, the old, kind King . . . (for though he was but
little past fifty years of age he seemed, because of the circumstances of his life, an old man) — the King who had treated her
kindly as if she were a little kitten, — he who had tried to make
her forget her unhappy childhood, and who had made her Queen.

What had she done to him, because of the fever left in her veins by the nights of her childhood ?

The frightful story continued, in all its pitiableness, its baseness. " She saith ", continued the Archbishop, " that Dereham used to her importune force, and had not her free will and consent."

So bit by bit, the whole story of that corrupted childhood came to light, through the pitying lips of the Archbishop, or divulged by voices shrieking under torture, or by comfortable voices gloating over the downfall of this unworthy creature who had seemed superior because of her birth, and who had been made Queen of England.

Chapter Fourteen

THINKING of her now, we see an unwanted child of thirteen, walking in the orchard at the back of the Duchess's house in Lambeth, with Henry Manox, a player on the virginals. We do not hear what they are saying for the wind has blown it away. . . . Or we see her, a young girl of fifteen, standing at the door of the waiting-women's sleeping apartment, which is also hers. . . . Night is falling. The old porter comes to lock the door and place the key in the Duchess's bedroom. . . . Silence . . . then the stolen key is fitted again in the lock, and somebody is admitted . . . one of the maids' lovers, or Katherine's.

Now she is standing, as we saw her in the previous chapter, in a shaft of sunlight, giving Francis Dereham a little ruby ring, that she would say, afterwards, in her examination, was "none of hers". . . . Or, perhaps, we are watching that dangerous stolen farewell between her and Dereham, before he fled from the Duchess's fury to become a pirate in Ireland. . . . Tears are streaming down Katherine's cheeks, and, in a broken voice, she is saying "Thou wilt never live to say I have swerved." . . . That summer day was long ago. . . . Or was it yesterday? . . . Dereham thought of it, as he lay in his prison. But Katherine, never. She hated Dereham, now, as much as she had once thought she loved him.

Katherine had been not quite thirteen years old when her mother died and she was sent to the old Duchess's house, to be relegated, there, to the companionship of the waiting-women, to spend the daylight hours with them, and her nights in their sleeping apartment.

These women were of an abandoned character, with a monkeyish chatter and a monkey's lubricity; and in these surroundings Katherine formed a childish fancy for Henry Manox. This horrible being, when he had obtained dominion over Katherine, was in the habit of indulging with this child —

(we must repeat, again, that she was but thirteen years old) — in an unspeakably lewd and frightful course of conduct, which cannot be described here ; and this he did in full view of the waiting-women.

Mary Lassels, the informer's sister, was told by Dorothy Barwicke, Katherine's confidante, that " Manox was troth-plight to Katherine ". Mary Lassels was a newcomer ; she seems to have felt hatred towards Katherine from the outset, — probably because she was the Duchess's granddaughter. She may, also, have felt jealousy, for she, too, may have had a fancy for Manox. In any case, according to her own account she reproached Manox violently, telling him " She is of a noble house, and if thou shalt marry her, some of her blood will kill thee ".

Manox replied, laughing, that his " designs were of a dishonest kind, and from the liberties the young lady had allowed him, he doubted not of being able to effect his purpose ".

When Katherine was told this by Mary Lassels, she was unable to restrain her anger, and going in search of Manox, to the house of Lord Beaumont, she there upbraided him passionately.

Once only after this was she seen in his company, walking with him at the back of the Duchess's orchard.

Then came the less frightful actual rape by Dereham, when Katherine was fifteen. But this child, an unwanted dependant, having no friends, being cared for neither by the Duchess nor the waiting-women, seems to have forgiven Dereham for his terrible act, because he was, in other ways, kind to her. . . . It must, by now, have meant so little to her, that violation. . . . And Dereham, in spite of his conduct, seems really to have loved her, in his benighted way. . . . Katherine drifted into consenting to become his " troth-plighted wife ".

Dereham called Katherine " wife " — though not in the presence of her family ; he gave all his money into her keeping ; he gave her little pieces of finery.

She had longed for an artificial flower, called a French fennel, which was fashionable among the ladies of Henry VIII's Court. She had not been able to afford one, but Dereham said he knew of " a little woman with a crooked back in London who could make these " ; and Katherine begged him to order and pay for one, saying she would repay him as soon as she could.

It was trivial matters such as this which helped to bring this ephemeral creature, this little wandering sun-mote, to her death ; and now it was on these that she concentrated, as though, if only the grave beings who were judging her could understand them, she, too, would be understood, and set free.

Her one idea, now, was to contradict all Dereham's statements ; and this made her insist, with " a peculiar childish obstinacy "[1] on certain points of no importance. For instance, it was said that Dereham had made her a present of a quilted cap, when she was " destitute of the means to make such a purchase ". " He bought not for me the quilted cap," said she, " but only the sarcenet to make it ; and I delivered the sarcenet to a little fellow in my lady's house to embroider (as I remember, his name was Rose) — to make it what pattern he thought best, and not appointing him to make it with friars' knots, as he can testify, if he be a true man." — Nevertheless, when it was made, Dereham said, " What, wife, here be friars' knots for Francis ".

This was a reference to a costume worn by the French King at the time of the Field of the Cloth of Gold.

In Hall's account there is this passage : " The French King and his band were apparelled in purple satin, branched with gold and purple velvet, embroidered with friars' knots, and in every knot was pansy flowers, which, together, signified ' Think on Francis ' ". (The Franciscans tied their girdles with the friars' knot.)

It was for this far-fetched reason that Dereham, whose first name was Francis, thought the friars' knots on the little quilted cap were a reference to him.

This poor child in her tawdry finery had certainly worn this cap, and the silk pansy that Dereham gave her.

She did what she listed. Nobody cared what became of her. " Let her alone," said Mary Lassels, " for if she hold on as she has begun, within a little while she will be naught."

The only care taken of her consisted in locking the door of the waiting-women's sleeping apartment, and placing the key in the Duchess's bedroom. But it was easy to steal the key.

" Sometimes," said Katherine, between her sobs, to the Council, " he " (Dereham) " would bring strawberries, apples, wine, and other things, to make good cheer with, after my lady was gone to bed ; but that he made any special banquet, or that, by special appointment between him and me, he should tarry till after the keys were delivered to my lady, is utterly untrue . . . but for many other causes the doors have been opened, and, sometimes, Dereham hath come early in the morning, and much misbehaved himself, but never by my request or consent."

Two of the women, under examination, declared that on one of these occasions it had been asked " what shifts should be made if my lady came suddenly in ? " and that Katherine replied, " Dereham must go into the little gallery if my lady come ". But Katherine denied this. " I never said so," she swore, " but he hath said it himself, and so hath he done, indeed."

The Duchess was very old, but nobody could be certain she would not appear unexpectedly. Once, coming suddenly into a room where the women sat embroidering, working at tapestry, or spinning, she found Katherine and Dereham, romping together in an unseemly, over-familiar fashion. She beat and buffeted them both, and gave Joan Bulmer a box on the ears for sitting by and permitting such conduct. Once an anonymous letter (written, Katherine believed, by Manox, who had shown signs of jealousy) told the Duchess of the nocturnal meetings. She stormed at her women, but seems to have taken no other steps, — though, when Dereham was not to be found, she would say, sardonically, " You shall find him in the maids' chamber, or with Katherine Howard ".

Yet, as Miss Strickland says, " she did not dismiss Dereham, because he was their relation, though she frequently chid the young lady, and sometimes punished her on his account ; but the tender age of Katherine appears to have blinded her as to the peril in which she stood ".

But at last, through one of the maids, the Duchess saw and " was forced to recognise the dreadful truth, with all its revolting circumstances ".[2]

Then, once again, she beat Katherine.

At the time of Katherine's examination, she was asked by

the Council of the King "whether the Duchess struck her on the discovery of her misconduct, and how often ". But there is no record of her reply.

Dereham fled, for he would have paid with his blood for the ruin of this daughter of the great family. And when he was gone, Katherine believed that her life was ended.

The story of her disgrace was hushed up, as far as the outward world was concerned ; but it was known to all the Duchess's household . . . the old porter and the groom of the chambers, according to the gloating Mary Lassels, " could tell much ".

She, and other beings of the same kind, had actually *witnessed* the corruption of the child who was now Queen of England : they had been present while it was done. . . . And on hearing this, the King hid his face in his hands. The Nessus-robe of flame clung round him. Perhaps these were the fires of damnation . . . and this was eternity . . . not time at all, not a few days and hours.

Tears rolled between his fingers, " a thing ", said an eye-witness, " much to be marvelled at in one of his courage ".

Sometimes the King's agony would turn to rage, and Marillac told the French King, " His love has turned to hatred ; and he has taken such grief at being deceived that of late it was thought he had gone quite mad, for he called for a sword to slay her whom he had loved so much. Sitting in council, he suddenly called for horses without saying where he would go. Sometimes he said irrelevantly that that wicked woman had never such delight in her incontinence as she should have torture in her death. And then took to tears."

But he could not outstrip, put to sleep, or melt to pity the ghost who must now be with him for ever. Anne Boleyn had returned from her grave, and looked at him through the re-membered eyes of the girl who must die because she had deceived him. The lineaments of that girl on the brink of death were those of the woman already dead, but more little, more light.

Doomed, like a moth, the terrified ephemeral creature brushed against the walls of her prison. But for her there was no escape.

She had no friends. The old Duchess, in terror, ransacked

the trunks and coffers Dereham had left in her house, lest any incriminating letters, documents which would bring her, also, to her death, might be found. She was sent to prison — as was Lord William Howard and his wife. The Duke of Norfolk did not share the family disgrace, but he walked with his head bowed, thinking of the sorrow his two nieces had brought upon his master. . . .

Intimate companions of Dereham were seized and put to the torture. One, named Dampier, under the torture of the Duke of Exeter's daughter (a brake which forced out the teeth), asked that he might speak with two gentlemen of the Council, and told these that Dereham had said to him, when the King first fell in love with "mistress Katherine", "I could be sure of Mistress Katherine Howard, an I would; but I dare not; the King beginneth to love her, but an he were dead I might marry her". . . . He said, too, that Dereham had told him that "the Duchess of Norfolk once said to a gentleman in the Queen's chamber, pointing to him, ' This is he who fled away to Ireland for the Queen's sake ' ".

But the informer Mary Lassels was not put to the torture. Not only was she exempted from the indictment for treason which fell on all the other witnesses of Katherine's corruption, but she received an intimation of his Majesty's gratitude to her for revealing this, and because " she did from the first opening of the matter to her brother seem to be sorry, and to lament that the King's majesty had married the Queen ".

Why did she make that revelation ? Because she had seen others offered places in the household of the Queen, while she received none ?

Alone, of all the people concerned, Dereham tried, by taking upon himself all the blame, by enduring extremities of torture rather than betray her, to save her from her fate. But Katherine by now hated him, as we have seen. She had been infected, in those frightful days and nights of her childhood, with an insatiable fever. And now her craving for Culpepper was as violent as it had ever been for Dereham. Culpepper, however, denied having any love for her, declaring that he had been dragged to his doom, swearing that it was the Queen, through Lady Rochford, who had solicited him to meet her in secret, when she told him she was dying for his love.

Lady Rochford, he swore, "contrived the interviews. The Queen would in every house seek for the back door and back stairs herself. At Pomfret she feared the King had set watch at the back door, and Lady Rochford made her servant watch in the court to see if this were so. . . . Once the Queen bade him beware if he went to confession, lest he should shrive him of any such things as should pass betwixt her and him; for if he did, surely, the King, being supreme head of the Church, should have knowledge of it." He had replied, "No, Madam, I warrant you." He added that "Lady Rochford provoked him much to love the Queen, and he intended to do ill with her ".[3]

On the 13th of November Katherine was removed as a prisoner to Sion House. Her attendants were summoned to the Star Chamber, and were there told of their mistress's disgrace. The household was then disbanded, the great ladies returning to their own homes, while Princess Mary was sent to the Palace of the baby Prince. . . . In this way the rumours spread, through the lips of mistress and maid.

The French Ambassador told his King that Katherine "refuses to drink or eat, and weeps and cries like a madwoman. As for Lady Rochford, on the third day of her imprisonment, she was seized with raving madness, and it was thought the same fate would befall the Queen." The frightful woman who had helped to encompass the death of her own husband and his sister "recovers her reason", Chapuys told the Emperor, "now and then; and the King gets his own physician to visit her, desiring her recovery that he may afterwards have her executed ".

Soon the Queen was sent from Sion House to the Tower.

"The Queen", it was announced in Parliament, on the 16th of January 1542, "has confederated with Lady Rochford, widow, to bring her vicious and abominable purpose to pass with Thos. Culpepper, late one of the King's Privy Chamber, and has met Culpepper in a secret and vile place at 11 o'clock at night, and remained there with him till 3 A.M. with only that bawd the Lady Rochford. For these treasons, Culpepper and Dereham have been attainted and executed, and the said Queen and Lady Rochford stand indicted."

Cranmer, out of pity, tried to induce Katherine to save her life by acknowledging a pre-contract with Dereham. She refused the offer with scorn. Only two requests did she make before her death. When the bill of attainder against the Queen was produced in the House of Lords, the Duke of Suffolk rose, and stated that he and his fellow deputies had been with the Queen, and that she had " openly confessed to them the great crime of which she had been guilty against the most high God and a kind prince, and lastly against the whole English nation ; that she begged of them all to implore his Majesty not to impute her crime to her whole kindred and family, but that his Majesty would extend his unbounded mercy and benevolence to her brothers, that they might not suffer for her faults. Lastly, she besought his Majesty, that it would please him to bestow some of her clothes on those maid-servants who had been with her from the time of her marriage, since she had now nothing else left to recompense them as they deserved." 4

The Commons then entered, and the sentence was pronounced, ending with the words " Le Roi le veut ".

There was now but little time left in which the shrieks of the Queen and the raving of the madwoman must be heard. On the 13th of February, these were heard for the last time. First the Queen, then Lady Rochford, were led to the block.

A rumour spread among the people that Katherine had said, with her dying lips, " I die Queen of England : but I would rather die the wife of Culpepper ". And this was repeated in the *Spanish Chronicle*. Actually the Queen, as Marillac told Francis I, " was so weak that she could hardly speak, but she confessed in a few words that she merited a hundred deaths ".

The tears shed by the giant, the fires that had consumed him, were gone. A short while afterwards, the French Ambassador told his master " The King inclines rather to keep his estates than to try his fortune in increasing them . . . much resembling his maternal grandfather, King Edward, being about his age, in loving rest and fleeing trouble. He seems very old and grey since the mishap of the last Queen, and will not hear of taking another. Although he is ordinarily in company of ladies, and his ministers beg and urge him to marry again."

The giant was crumbling under the shadow of his doom, though he was to take one more wife, and with her, to know a certain amount of happiness.

But the days of his physical vigour were gone. " The King ", wrote Burnet,[5] " was overgrown with corpulency, so that he became more and more unwieldy. He could not go up and down stairs but as he was raised up and let down by an engine. The fistula in his leg gave him ceaseless pain, and his rages were therefore increased in violence and more frequent."

According to Lingard, " the succession was repeatedly altered, and at last left to the King's private judgment and affections. It was once treason to dispute, and afterwards treason to maintain, the validity of the marriage of Anne Boleyn, and the legitimacy of her daughter. It became treason to marry, without the royal license, any of the King's children, whether legitimate or natural, his paternal brothers or sisters, or their issue, or for any woman to marry the King unless she were a maid, or had previously revealed to him her former incontinence. It was treason to call the King a heretic or schismatic, openly to wish him harm, or to slander him, his wife, or his issue. Nor was this all. The King had a right to tear the thoughts out of a man's breast. He could extort from him his secret sentiments upon oath, and subject him to the penalty of treason if those sentiments did not accord with the royal pleasure."

His servants spoke to him with fear, lest they should say anything which could remind him of his approaching end. " For ", said Burnet,[6] " an Act of Parliament had been passed for the security of his life ; in which there was a clause condemning the foretelling of his death ; and nobody could tell if the King, invaded by some angry and imperious humours, might not order them to be condemned under this statute."

The King, gradually, was surrounded by silence.

NOTES TO CHAPTER FOURTEEN

[1] See Strickland, *Katherine Howard*.   (Lives of the Queens of England.)
[2] *Ibid.*
[3] Confession of Thomas Culpepper.
[4] Lingard, *Journals of Parliament.*
[5] Burnet, *History of the Reformation.*
[6] *Ibid.*

Chapter Fifteen

THE young man with a giant's stature and "the face of an angel", with a beard which "had the appearance of being of gold", was now an old man waiting for death.

Long past were the days when the spectators, watching "a most stately joust" between the King and his brother-in-law, the Duke of Suffolk, fancied they were "witnessing a joust between Hector and Achilles". The man whom Erasmus had called "a universal genius", the great King of whose character, as a young man, "tolerance and clemency were no small part", was now a mountain of pain, waiting for dissolution.

On this warm day at the end of January 1547, a new life seemed almost to spring from the mould. In the gardens of Westminster, and those that surrounded the Palace of Hampton Court, to whose walls, the colour of a bullfinch's rosy feathers, plaited rosemary was nailed, — the roots of sweet-williams, violets, primroses, "gillyvor slips" and mints, lay hidden under the manure of strawberry-rot.

"For December and January", wrote a great man [1] who lived in the reign of Henry's younger daughter, "you must take such things as are green all winter : Holly, Ivy, Bays, Juniper, Cypress Trees, Yews, Pine Apple Trees, Fir Trees, Rosemary, Lavender, Periwinckles, the White, the Purple, and the Blue, Germander, Flags, Orange Trees, Lemon Trees and Myrtles, if they be warm set."

All these had been planted by the orders of the King that they might give pleasure to Anne Boleyn. But now this warm life, like her own, lay silent. And the little dark warm airs drifted through the gardens and the palace, listening at doors, floating around until they came to the room with the great bed of red satin and gold.

But the King was no longer there. He had left Hampton Court and had gone to die at Whitehall, in the heart of his capital.

Some months before, the King had addressed his people in Parliament, for the last time, and in the tones of a wicked father who had yet loved his children. " He spoke ", said Sir John Mason, " so sententiously, so kingly, or rather fatherly." [2] . . . The present, he said, was not the first time the people had showed their love to him : they knew that, as their hearts were turned toward him, so was his heart towards them. . . . He paused — his voice trembled . . . then tears rained down his cheeks.

He spoke to them of charity between Christians . . . ". . . be in charity one with another," he said, " like brother and sister. Have respect to the pleasing of God, and then I doubt not that love I spake of shall never be dissolved betwixt us. Then may I firstly rejoice that thus long I have lived to see this day, and you, by verity, conscience, and charity between yourselves, may be, in this point, as you be in divers others, accounted among the rest of the world as blessed men."

He spoke no more, but, says Froude, " passed down from the throne and departed ".

He knew now that he was about to leave his people. Soon, they would have no tyrannical father to force them to a good behaviour, and, by his own strength of will and foresight, avert the dangers that threatened them — the wars and internal upheavals. . . .

But he still had the strength to send a message which would cast a deathly chill over his old enemy and friend, the King of France. — Granvelle was told by his correspondent St. Mauris (21st March) that " a message had been received by the King of France from the King of England on his death-bed, bidding him remember that he, too, was mortal ".

This had so disturbed the King of France that he fell ill from that moment. François de Guise, watching him, had exclaimed, " Il s'en va, le vieux galant ! "

And, in effect, he died on the 30th of March, two months after the death of the English King.

The accounts given of Henry's death by Catholics and Protestants are diametrically opposed.

At the time of his dying, according to the priest, Harpsfield, terrors and visions beset the King. With " looks of wild import, he glared at the darker recesses of the kingly bedchamber . . . and he would mutter to himself ' Monks . . . Monks.' . . . "

If this is true — what did this dying man see ? The last moments of the gentle monks of the Charterhouse, as they were disembowelled and their hearts were torn from their bodies ? Or from his Nessus-robe of flame, and the fires that burned in the fistula upon his leg and in his corrupted veins, did he see the fires that consumed, seven years before this time, Richard Mekins, a " child not past his fifteenth year ", — burned to death at Smithfield for heresy, because, according to Hall's *Chronicle*, " he had heard folkes talke, and in his innocence had chanced to speak against the Sacrament of the Altar. . . . The poore boy for the safeguard of his life would gladly have said that the twelve apostles taught it hym " (the heresy) " for he had not cared whom he had named . . . such was his childish innocence and feare."

But the primary guilt of that enormity lay with Bonner, who had " delightedly followed the accusation and found the means to indite him ". So perhaps the thought of those flames did not add to the torment of the dying King.

The account given of his death by those near him, and also the Protestants, was very different from that given by Harpsfield : it told how, warned that his end was near, the King considered his past life ; which, although he had " much abused it, yet, said he, is the mercy of Christ able to pardon all my sins, though they were greater than they be ".

At times he would sleep for a while, or fall into unconsciousness. Then, growing worse, he expressed a wish to see the Archbishop. But when Cranmer arrived, the King was already past speech. . . . Cranmer, " speaking comfortably to him, desired him to give some token that he put his trust in God through Jesus Christ ; therewith the King wrung hard the Archbishop's hand, and expired ".[3]

Thus, at three o'clock in the morning of the 27th of January 1547, " this most miserable of Princes, cursed in the extinction of his race, as if God would punish those distracted marriages from which, in spite of fortune, he laboured to beget sons to succeed him ", was alone, save for the silence.

But at first there was no sign given to the outer world of the King's new companionship. Even the royal ceremony of bearing in the King's dishes to the noise of trumpets was continued. Van Der Delft, who had succeeded Chapuys as Imperial Ambassador, could not convey the news to the Emperor until the 31st of January, because " all the roads were closed ".

In the King's last years, he had led a comparatively calm domestic life with his latest wife, Katherine Parr, a happy-natured, placid woman, with hair as bright golden as the marsh-marigolds of spring, and with some pretensions to learning. She had already been married, twice, to elderly husbands. The first of these, Lord Borough, left her a widow when she was fifteen years of age ; the second, Lord Latimer, had not been in his grave for many months before the King decided to make her his new Queen.

Katherine Parr was now thirty-four years of age, and she proved an admirable nurse and companion to her new husband, and a perfect stepmother to his children, by whom she was much loved. She induced the King to have the neglected Elizabeth brought to Court, and given an apartment at Whitehall next to her own rooms.⁴ Her influence on the little Prince was such that his handwriting bore a childish resemblance to hers. Mary, in spite of their religious differences — Katherine was a fervent Protestant — was her devoted friend. — The new stepmother interceded for them, when they were in disgrace with the King: for example, there is a letter from Elizabeth to the Queen, dated from St. James, the 31st of July 1544, which shows that she had been forgiven for some fault or other, owing to her stepmother's intercession. . . .

In the same summer, Elizabeth wrote a letter in Italian addressed to her stepmother, and began a translation into English of Margaret Queen of Navarre's *Le Miroir de l'Âme Pécheresse*. This " godlye medytacyon of the Christian soule concerning a love towards God and His Christe, compyled by the right ver-tuouse Lady Elizabeth " was presented to the Queen as a New Year's gift. " The embroidered binding (wrote Mr. de la Mare in the Notes to *Come Hither*) has K — P in the centre, and this is surrounded by a diamond-shaped design with four flowers of heartsease embroidered at the corners."

The eleven-year-old Elizabeth seems to have taken a gloomy view of this literary work, saying that " it is all imperfect and incorrect ", and that " having joined the sentences together as well as the capacity of her simple wit and small learning could extend themselves, she knows it was many places rude, and nothing done as it should be ".[5]

No doubt, however, the Queen found much to please her in it.

Once only did the King's admirable new wife forget the precept laid down by her in her " Lamentations of a Sinner ", in which (after comparing the King to Moses delivering the people from the bondage of Pharaoh — " by which I meane the Bishop of Rome ") she had urged all married women to " learn of St. Paul to be obedient to their husbands, and to keep silence in the congregation and to learn of their husbands at home ". She actually contradicted His Grace in some matter of doctrine, and he, suffering from the pain of the fistula, was heard by Bishop Gardiner to mutter " a good hearing it is, when women become such clerks ; and much to my comfort, to come in my old age to be taught of my wife ".

This was an opportunity not to be missed ; for the Queen's tenets were inconvenient to Gardiner. " It was unseemly ", he declared, " for any of his " (the King's) " subjects to argue with him so malapertly as the Queen had just done. That it was grievous for any of his Counsellors to hear it done, since those who were so bold in words would not scruple to proceed to acts of disobedience ", — adding " that he would make great discoveries if he were not deterred by the Queen's powerful faction ". In short, " he crept so far into the King at that time ", according to Foxe, " that he gave them warrant to consult together about drawing of articles against the Queen, wherein her life might be touched. They thought it best to begin with such ladies as she most esteemed, and were privy to all her doings, — as the Lady Herbert, afterwards Countess of Pembroke, her sister ; the Lady Jane, who was her first cousin ;

and the lady Tyrwhit, all of her privy chamber ; and to accuse
them of the six articles, and to search their closets and coffers,
that they might find somewhat to charge the Queen ; which,
being found, the Queen should be taken and carried by night
to the Tower, of which advice the King was made privy by
Gardiner."

That is Foxe's version. The story continues that the Queen,
at first, was unconscious of any threatened danger. But, by
chance, a paper was picked up in a gallery by one of the attendants. This paper was the mandate for her arrest, and it
had been dropped by Wriothesley, who was one of the principals
in the plot against her.

On seeing this paper, the Queen retired to her apartments,
which were next to those of the King. Here she screamed so
loudly and so incessantly that at last the King, " incommoded
by the noise ", could stand it no longer, and had himself wheeled
into her Majesty's apartments, where an affecting reconciliation
took place. The Queen assured her husband that she had only
argued in order to try to distract his mind from the pain of his
illness, and " in the hope of profiting by your Majesty's dis-
course ". On hearing this, the King embraced her tenderly,
saying " Is it so, sweetheart ? Then are we perfect friends." [6]

The next day being fine, and the King convalescent, he sent
for the Queen to sit with him in the garden. . . . As the royal
pair sat, enjoying the air and the beauty and scent of the flowers,
Wriothesley appeared, with forty of the guard, to take the
Queen to the Tower — (for this was the day appointed for her
arrest). He met with a most unexpected reception. The King,
half rising from his chair, greeted him with roars of " Beast ",
" Knave ", and " Blockhead ", — ordering him not to dare
approach the Queen, and finally bidding him " avaunt from
our presence ".

The gentle Queen then said she would intercede for the
chancellor, — would " become a humble suitor for him, as she
deemed his fault was occasioned by mistake ".

" Ah, poor soul," said the King, " thou little knowest, Kate,
how evil he deserveth this grace at thy hands. On my word,
sweetheart, he hath been to thee a very knave."

His Majesty never forgave his chancellor.

The calm domestic life was resumed, and when the pain of the fistula was particularly bad, his Majesty would lay his leg upon his wife's lap.

Peace at last. Happiness — or a kind of happiness, at last.

But the patient nurse and companion of the King, and of two elderly husbands before him, was soon to be released from her labours. She was learned and pious, and in learning and piety she had found her only distractions. But now it seemed to her as if she had come out of a dark and cold room where someone lay dying, into the sunlight. She had a happy nature, as bright as that hair which was like the kingcups of spring, — she was fond of laughter, affectionate and warm-hearted, and she told herself that she was still young — thirty-five : she was Queen-Dowager, and the world lay before her. By the world, she meant love.

Now, as she took charge of her stepdaughter Elizabeth, who, with her governess Mrs. Katherine Ashley, and her household, had been sent, on the King's death, to the Queen's country palace at Chelsea, the stepmother's thoughts were for herself, — perhaps for the first time in her life.

For herself, and for one other, — a being whom she had loved years ago, before it was her duty to become Queen of England.

NOTES TO CHAPTER FIFTEEN

[1] Francis Bacon, *On the Making of Gardens.*
[2] Mason to Paget, Froude, *Henry VIII.*
[3] Strype's *Cranmer* ; Froude, *Henry VIII.*
[4] Mumby, *The Girlhood of Queen Elizabeth.*
[5] Hearne's *Sylloge.*
[6] Foxe's *Book of Martyrs* ; Lingard ; Herbert of Cherbury.

Chapter Sixteen

TOWARDS the end of their father's life, the heir to the throne and his sister Elizabeth had lived for the most part at Hatfield, sharing many of their lessons. Elizabeth was under the charge of Mrs. Ashley ; Edward, either then, or a little later, had as tutor the learned Mr. Cheke. They were taught French by one Jean Balmain ; Elizabeth alone was given lessons in Italian by Battisti Castiglioni.

The education of Elizabeth must have been much on the lines laid down for the education of her sister Mary by the learned Ludovicus Vives (called by his contemporaries, the second Quintilian).

" His rules ", said Miss Strickland,[1] " were rigid : the Princess must read no idle books of chivalry or romance, such as *Don Quixote*, *Lancelot du Lac*, or *Pierre Provençal*. Instead, she must read the Gospels at night, and in the morning, the Acts of the Apostles, the Epistles, selected passages from the Old Testament, and the works of St. Cyprian, St. Jerome, St. Augustine, and St. Ambrose, — Plato, Cicero, Seneca's *Maxims*, Plutarch's *Enchiridion*, the *Paraphrase* of Erasmus, and the *Utopia* of Sir Thomas More. Among the works of the classic poets, the *Pharsalia* of Lucan, and the tragedies of Seneca might be admitted, with carefully selected portions of Horace. . . . A few stories might be permitted for the Princess's relaxation, but these must all have a purely historical, sacred, or classic basis. — The one exception to this rule was the not over-exciting tale of Griselda ; but apart from that the story of Joseph and his Brethren was a good example of the tales chosen for the Princess's amusement."

Elizabeth's education must have been on the same lines. Both she and Edward had a natural leaning towards learning.

" So pregnant and ingenuous were they either," wrote Sir John Hayward, an historian living at the end of Elizabeth's reign, " that they desired to look upon books as soon as the day began to break. Their *horae matutinae* were so welcome that they seemed to prevent the night's sleeping for the entertainment of the morrow's schooling. Besides, such were the hopeful indications of this princely youth and pious virgin, that their first hours were spent in prayer and religious exercises as either reading some history or other in the Old Testament, or else attending the exposition of some text or other in the New." (The princely youth was at the time eight — or nine at the most, — the pious virgin twelve, or thirteen.) " The rest of the forenoon (breakfast excepted) they were doctrinated and instructed either in language or some of the literal sciences or moral learning or other, collected out of such authors as did best conduce to the instruction of Princes. And when he was called out to any youthful exercises becoming a child of his age (for study without action breeds dullness), she, in her private chamber betook herself to her lute or viol, and wearied with that, to practise her needle. This was the circular course of their employment. God was the centre of all their actions."

Neither Elizabeth nor Edward was present at the death of their father, nor were they together at that time. In the winter of 1546, Edward was sent to Hertford, and Elizabeth to the Palace at Enfield. The two children exchanged letters in Latin, and the first the Princess received from her brother, a strange wintry little note, yet with a certain childish warmth showing through the formality, ran thus (in the translation) :

" Change of place, in fact, does not vex me so much, dearest sister, as your going from me. Now, however, nothing can happen more agreeable to me than a letter from you, and especially as you are the first to send a letter to me, And have challenged me to write. . . . But this is some comfort to my grief, that I hope to visit you shortly (if no accident interfere with either me or you) as my chamberlain hath reported to me.

Farewell, dearest sister

Edward the Prince."

They were to meet under very different circumstances than they expected. Very early one morning, Edward the Prince was awakened and taken to join his sister that they might be together when they were told of their father's death.

The nine-year-old King and the thirteen-year-old Princess wept so bitterly that their attendants burst into tears.

That Edward should weep was natural — his father had always shown him tenderness. But why did Elizabeth shed such abundant tears ? Perhaps she held the old King in some affection — it is possible that she believed the stories of her mother's guilt, and that Henry was as deeply injured as he was unhappy. Perhaps — for she was a child of strange insight, who could then, as later in life, " see into the hearts of men ", she understood, even at that early age, the Atridean doom of the man who had brought her into being. Now he had gone, and the whole of her life was changed, at thirteen.

> King Pandion he is dead,
> All thy friends are lapped in lead.

Her life was altered in more ways than one, for she was now a Princess once again : her father had reinstated her and her sister Mary in the succession to the Crown.

In any case, whatever was the reason for Elizabeth's tears, they were soon dried, and her brother wrote to her : " Your letter was very pleasant to me, both for the charming thoughts that it contained, and because I see in it with what evenness of mind you have borne our father's death ".

Had they but known it, the two children, as they clung together, weeping, were saying farewell to each other, as to their childhood.

We saw those children, from time to time, in the letters of their tutors, or some other person of their households, entering a room, opening a door and passing through it, speaking a few words in a youthful voice. But that is all : of their real thoughts we had no idea. Now, suddenly, these will be revealed to us.

Elizabeth was no longer the lion-willed baby who had been the pride and despair of Lady Bryane. Schooled to caution, to watch every movement lest it should be on the brink of danger, this thirteen-year-old girl, in whose flat childish body the spring was beginning to stir, was about to undergo a new peril.

Edward, too, had changed, and not in appearance only ;

and Elizabeth must have known this, as she looked at him by the new light of his kingship. When he was a baby he had had a round face like a great rosy apple ; his straight fox-coloured hair was thick. He had looked very grand, when, aged two years, he wore the little coat of crimson satin Princess Mary had ordered to be made for him, embroidered with gold by the King's broiderers, and with pansies made of great pearls — with tinsel sleeves and four large aglets or hooks of gold.

But now he was grander still, for he was King of England.

But his apple-round cheeks had grown thin and pale ; his hair, too, was thin as a crane's feathers ; and he had a sly look.

This strange, cold child, begot to be a King, doomed to an early death, had, perhaps, a little affection for his sister Elizabeth. Mary was so much older that she belonged to another world ; and the only people he seems to have really loved were Mother Jack, his nurse, and his " whipping-boy ", — the child who was his constant companion, and who, when Edward was naughty, was punished in his stead.

The King was a secretive child, and showed little of his mind, excepting on those occasions when secretiveness would give place to a devastating candour. He inherited much of his father's shrewdness ; and, when one of his Ministers, pleading the cause of a criminal, said he had only stolen a little money, replied, " But he would have *liked* it to be more ".

We see him in a more pleasant light in his friendship with Jane Dormer, afterwards the Duchess of Feria, whom he called " My Jane ", when they were six years old, and played cards together. " Now Jane," the Prince would say, " your king is gone, and I shall be good enough for you."

But now the days of games were over, and the forlorn little boy must listen to Bishop Latimer's interminable sermons, when he was not attending to affairs of state. In one of these sermons the Bishop complained that the people had preferred Robin Hood to himself. " Sir," they had said, " this is a busy day for us. We cannot hear you, it is Robin Hood's Day. . . . The parish are gone abroad to gather for Robin Hood. . . . I thought my rocket " (*i.e.* Bishop's vestment) " should have been regarded. . . . But it would not serve, it was fain to give place to Robin Hood's men. It is no laughing matter, my friends, it is a weeping matter."

So he droned on and on, like an angry bee buzzing round the branches gathered for that man of the woods.

Laughing matters were, indeed, over for the nine-year-old Edward. To him, even his sisters must kneel, whenever they addressed him. He must listen to Bishop Latimer for hours on end, and must not listen to Robin Hood for a moment. He was King, but he was also a little boy who was not allowed enough pocket-money.

And now a new ghost was to walk across the path of Elizabeth — a ghost with a physical manifestation — a strong-voiced, gallant, swashbuckling man, thirty-eight years of age : Admiral Lord Seymour of Sudeley, the brother of Edward's mother and of the Duke of Somerset who was now Protector of England.

This ghost, who opened the eyes of Elizabeth to a spring world of beauty, of flowering, and panic danger, was to haunt Elizabeth for the rest of time.

His conduct affected her whole life : it blasted her reputation for ever in the eyes of certain people.

"It was afterwards believed", wrote Lingard, "that her licentious habits survived, even when the fires of wantonness had been quenched by the chill of age." The Court imitated the manners of the sovereign. It was a place in which, according to Faunt, "all enormities reigned in the highest degree", or, as Harington said, "where there was no love, but that of the lusty god Asmodeus".

This base slander upon Elizabeth originated, the present writer believes, in the stories about the Admiral's behaviour towards her when she was a child of thirteen or fourteen years.

The characters of the two Seymour brothers were strongly opposed. . . . "The Admiral", according to Heylin,[2] "was fierce in courage, courtly in fashion, in personage stately, in voice magnificent, but somewhat empty of matter. The Duke was mild, affable, free and open, more easily to be worked on, but in no way malicious, and honoured by the common people, as the Admiral was more generally esteemed among the nobler. The Protector was more to be desired as a friend, and the other more to be feared as an enemy. The defects of each being taken away, the virtues united would have made an excellent man."

That magnificent personage, the Admiral, fell into a fury when he realised that his elder, more cautious brother was to be Protector of the Kingdom. . . . So open was his resentment, that he was reminded by Lord Warwick, in extremely strong language, accompanied by threats, that he had come to occupy his own high position simply through the favour of his brother and the Council, who had admitted him against the wish of the late King, who, on his death-bed, hearing the Admiral's name among those elected to the Council, cried out "No, No," though his breath was failing.

Warwick's threats were so effectual that the Admiral went at once and patched up his quarrel with his brother. But the hatred in his soul, the envy, grew.

Was he not also the uncle of the King ? Was one brother only to profit by the relationship ?

No sooner was King Henry dead than the Admiral determined to marry Elizabeth, although she was then only thirteen years and four months old. In this plan he was " stayed " by the Protector and the Council, but Mrs. Katherine Ashley, the Princess's governess, heard the rumours. "I told the Lord Admiral at the Park at St. James that I heard one say he should have married my lady Elizabeth," she said in her depositions, after the arrest of the Admiral. — " Nay," says he, " I love not to lose my life for a wife. It has been spoken of, but it cannot be." [3]

Thwarted in this plan, the Admiral made up his mind to influence events in another way. He urged that Princess Mary should be sent to the Tower. When this benevolent suggestion was not acted upon, he changed his mind, and asked his brother's permission to marry the lady whom he had wished to be imprisoned — receiving in reply a sharp rebuke for his presumption.

But the Admiral was not yet at the end of his matrimonial plans.

Before the late King's last marriage, he, Admiral Seymour, had nearly become the husband of the lately widowed Lady

Latimer. Then his brother-in-law, the King, intervened, and the widow became Queen of England. But the Admiral, with his gambler's instinct, knew that the feeling she had for him was not dead.

Lord Seymour of Sudeley seemed, to his companions, to be in a thoughtful mood.

Shortly after this last interview with his brother, in which he asked permission to marry Princess Mary, he, half jokingly, sent one Fowler, a gentleman of the King's household, with a message to be delivered secretly to the child, asking him who he would like his uncle to marry. . . . The pale, secretive little boy replied instantly, " The lady Anne of Cleves," — then pausing for a moment, he added, " Nay, nay, know you what? I would he married my sister Mary, to turn her opinions." Then, Fowler told the Admiral, " his Highness went about his ways, and said no more at the time ".

But the Admiral was not satisfied, and meeting Fowler in a gallery at St. James's Palace, said, " I pray you, Mr. Fowler, ask the King's grace if he should be contented I should marry the Queen . . . in case I should be a suitor to his Highness for a letter to the Queen, whether he would write for me or not."

Afterwards, the Admiral succeeded in seeing the boy alone for a few moments.

In fact, the younger Seymour brother proposed to mount over the head of the elder by marrying the late King's widow; he determined also to obtain a hold over the mind of the little boy who was now King, through the very secrecy of his understanding with him.

Meanwhile, he urged the Queen to marry him without the permission of the Protector and the Council.

The date of this secret marriage is unknown, but Katherine certainly became the Admiral's wife very shortly after the death of the old King. She whose life had been devoted to doing her duty, obeying the precepts of her religious teachers, wrote to her old suitor :

" I would not have you to think this mine honest good will toward you to proceed of any sudden motion of passion; for as truly as God is my God, my mind was fully bent, the other time I was at liberty, to marry you before any man I knew. Howbeit God withstood my will therein most vehemently for a time, and through his grace and goodness made that possible which seemed to me most impossible ; that was, made me renounce utterly mine own will, and to follow his will most willingly. . . . As my lady of Suffolk saith, 'God is a marvellous man.'

"By her that is yours to serve and obey during her life

Katheryn the Quene, K.P.

"Enclosed. The Queen's letter from Chelsea to my lord admiral . . . of her former loves."

The Queen, in this, the first real happiness of her life, knew nothing of her husband's thwarted attempts to marry the thirteen-year-old Elizabeth, to marry Mary. Nor had any whisper reached her of a young woman of whom Latimer spoke in his sermon preached before the King after the Admiral's execution — a young woman who had been seduced and then deserted by the Admiral, and who, in her destitution, fell into crime and was executed. . . .

Soon the Queen was admitting her new husband, secretly, at night, to the Palace at Chelsea. . . . "When it shall be your pleasure to repair thither," she wrote, "you must take some pain to come early in the morning, that ye may be gone again by seven o'clock ; and so I suppose you may come without suspect. I pray you let me have knowledge, over night, at what hour ye will come, that your portress may wait in the fields for you. . . ."

At this time Elizabeth was living in the Palace at Chelsea with her stepmother. . . . She must have known, — or may have known — of those nocturnal meetings ; but she did not know that the Queen was the Admiral's wife. — Katherine Howard had been executed for her lewd conduct when Elizabeth was eight years old. . . . There were the stories of her own mother, and her death as proof that they were true. And now Katherine Parr, who had appeared to her as goodness itself, had gone the same way. . . . There is no one in whose virtue you may believe. . . . All is falseness . . . all is pretence. . . .

Having succeeded in his plan to marry the Queen, Seymour now set about devising a way in which the marriage should be made public. His wife suggested he should apply to the Council. . . . " If the Duke " (of Somerset) "and the Duchess do not like the marriage," she declared, "it would be of no consequence."

The Admiral sought the approval of Princess Mary, and received, in reply, an appalling snub veiled by sweetness. . . .

After thanking him, charmingly, for several letters, she wrote, " I perceive strange news concerning you and a suit you have in hand to the Queen for marriage, for the sooner obtaining thereof you seem to think that my letters might do you a favour.

" My lord, in this case I trust your wisdom doth consider that of all creatures in the world it standeth least with my poor honour to be a meddler in this matter. Considering whose wife her Grace was of late. And besides that, if she be minded to grant your suit, my letters shall do you but small pleasure. On the other side, if the remembrance of the King's majesty my father (whose soul God pardon) will not suffer her to grant your suit, I am nothing able to persuade her to forget the loss of him who is as yet very rife in my own remembrance. Whereof I shall most earnestly require you (the premises considered) to think none unkindness in me, though I refuse to be a meddler in any ways in this matter, assuring you that (wooing matters set apart, wherein, being a maid, I am nothing cunning) if otherwise it shall lie in my power to do you pleasure, I shall be as glad to do it as you to require it, both for his blood's sake that you be of, and also for the gentleness I have always found in you, as knoweth Almighty God, to whose tuition I commend you."

As a result of letters delivered secretly by Fowler to the King, the little boy, however, was induced to favour the marriage, and even to believe it was of his own making, for he wrote this letter to his stepmother, with his own hand :

" To the Queen's Grace.

" We thank you heartily, not only for the gentle acceptation of our suit moved unto you, but also for the loving accomplishing

of the same, wherein you have declared a desire to gratify us.
. . . Wherefore ye shall not need to fear any grief to come or
to suspect lack of aid in need, seeing that he, being mine uncle,
is of so good a nature that he will not be troublesome any means
unto you, and I of such mind, that for divers just causes I must
favour you. . . .

"I will so provide for you both, that if hereafter any grief
befall, I shall be a sufficient succour in your godly and praisable
enterprises.

"Fare ye well, with much increase of honour and virtue in
Christ. From St. James, the five and twenty day of June.

Edward."

But the King who thus extended his protection was only
a little boy, and his views on his stepmother's re-marriage
were not shared by the Protector of the realm.

The marriage was discovered, and the King wrote in his
Journal : " My Lord Protector was much displeased ".

For the marriage had followed so soon after the death of
the late King, that fresh complications might have arisen about
the succession.

NOTES TO CHAPTER SIXTEEN

[1] Strickland, *Mary I.*
[2] Heylin, *History of the Reformation.*
[3] Depositions of Katherine Ashley, *Domestic Papers Edward VI*, vol. vi.

Chapter Seventeen

IN the long galleries and state apartments of the Palace of Westminster, a little boy to whom everyone must kneel, complained of his hard lot, his absence of pocket-money.

That complaint was soon to be modified.

"My uncle Somerset," the child declared, "deals so hard with me and keeps me so strait, that I cannot have money at my will. But my lord Admiral both sends me money and gives me money." The Admiral told John Fowler, that gentleman of the King who had already proved useful, "If his highness lacked any money, to send to him for it, and to nobody else".

Of this generous offer the boy took full advantage.

The Admiral spent much of his time at the Palace, " lounging " (to use Froude's description) negligently in the galleries, looking out of the windows idly, waiting for news.

War had broken out between England and Scotland, and the Protector had gone to Scotland with the army. But the Admiral, who seems to have been strangely indulged by his brother, in spite of their underground dissension, had calmly refused to take charge of the fleet that was to land the army on Scottish soil. He remained in England, ostensibly in order to superintend the preparations that were being made against a possible invasion by the French, but at the same time utilising his opportunities to cultivate each personal advantage.

The Admiral was a gambler, and he took gamblers' risks. He understood that now was the time to gain an influence over his nephew, and he watched for any opportunity of the kind. But for all his watchfulness, there was one thing that he did not understand, and that was to help bring him to the scaffold. It never entered his head that the ten-year-old King was watching him with an understanding that far outmatched his own. When the King looked at him unwaveringly, the Admiral saw a small boy admiring a brave, swashbuckling, worldly-wise, generous uncle — a donor of pocket-money. He did not guess that a

King was watching, with complete comprehension, a scheming but stupid, troublesome subject. He did not dream that silence, or a few non-committal words on the part of this small boy, meant anything but an absence of thought. The uncle condescended to his nephew, took him into his confidence; and the presents of pocket-money gave the Admiral a pleasant sense that there was a secret understanding between them.

The Admiral was very candid on the subject of the Protector's lack of wisdom, and harshness. . . . "As for the invasion of Scotland," he told-the child, "it was a disastrous mistake . . . the money spent on it was thrown away, and not only would the Protector lose his own life, but the Army would suffer immense losses."

The small boy stared up at him with unblinking eyes.

Under his gaze, the Admiral grew more expansive. "You are too bashful," he told the boy patronisingly. "Why do ye not speak to have rule as others do? You must take it upon yourself to rule, for ye shall be able enough, as well as other kings. . . . And then you may give your men somewhat."

Afterwards, when the Admiral was brought to trial, Edward, with one of his devastating bursts of candour, repeated to the Council another part of that conversation: "'Your uncle,' said the Admiral, 'is old and I trust will not live long.' I answered, 'It were better he should die'.

"Then he" (the Admiral) "said, 'Ye are but a beggarly king now; ye have not' (money with which) 'to play or to give to your servants'. I said, 'Mr. Stanhope had money for me'. Then he said he would give Fowler money for me. Fowler often said to me, 'You must thank my lord Admiral for gentilnes that he showed you, and for his money' — and he was always praising him."

The Protector returned to England, and the pocket-money had to be given in greater secrecy. At the time of the Admiral's trial for treason, this note was found on a slip of paper. . . . "My lord, I thank you, and pray you to have me remembered to your Quene. Edward." — And another piece of paper, torn off a sheet, was also found, with this message: "My lord, send me for Latimer as much as ye think good".

For the virtuous Bishop Latimer, who railed with such indignation at the infamy of the Admiral, when that infamy had brought him to the block, must be paid by the King for his sermons, and the money for that payment came from this tainted source.

The above message was sent from Hampton on the 18th of July. On the following day, Fowler wrote to the Admiral : " I write unto you, if his grace could get any spare time, his grace would write a letter to the Queen's grace and to you, but his highness desires you to pardon him, for he is not half an hour alone." . . . He added : " he is so much bounden to you that he must remember you always ".

He did. And his remembrance was both full and fatal. Everything that the Admiral had ever said to the King was repeated, at the time of the Admiral's trial, by the little boy whom he had thought to bribe with pocket-money.

The Admiral's ambition, fed by his marriage to the Queen, grew greater. Before the meeting of the first Parliament of the reign, he complained to several persons that the late King had never intended that there should be a Protector, or, at least, if one uncle was regent of the realm, it was intended that the other should have the custody of the King's person. For to obtain this custody was the Admiral's real aim. He had a Bill drawn up, separating the two offices, and tried to induce Sir John Cheke, the King's tutor, to make the boy copy and sign it. But Cheke refused, and the astute child who was his pupil, replied, " If the thing was right, the Lords would allow it, if it was ill he would not meddle with it."

The Bill came to nothing ; but the Admiral was unabashed. Indefatigable in his attempts to circumvent every plan of the Protector (who had determined to marry his own daughter to the King, and his son to Lady Jane Grey, a possible heiress to the throne) ; the Admiral purchased the wardship of Lady Jane from her father, Lord Dorset, with a promise that should she live in his house, he would " match her much to his (her father's) comfort ".

Lord Dorset enquired to whom she should be married. " I doubt not," he was assured by the gentleman sent to effect the transaction, " you shall see him marry her to the King."

That watchful little boy noted, with dignified displeasure, in his Journal, this presumptuous attempt on the part of his uncle to marry him to a subject — observing that he intended, on the contrary, to choose as his queen " a foreign princess, well stuffed and jewelled ".

The King, meanwhile, was not the Admiral's only confidant. He had others, almost equally dangerous. In his capacity as Lord High Admiral, he had been brought into contact with certain pirates — men who were an admixture of the later ferocious Captain Yallahs, or Yellows, and of the Elizabethan adventurers. It was the Admiral's duty to punish these malefactors and to return the booty they had seized to the owners. He did nothing of the kind. When, soon after King Henry's death, Thompson of Calais, one of the chief pirates, seized the Scilly Isles and held them as a base for his operations, the Admiral was sent with a large force to dislodge him. But Thompson remained in the islands. And afterwards, it was noticed that the Admiral's followers were in possession of some of the missing booty.[1] The truth was that the Admiral had compacted with Mr. Thompson to share the control of Lundy Island, and to divide the pirates' profits ! — He imprisoned persons bringing charges against his new friends, he levied blackmail on ships. . . . . France complained, the Ambassador of the Emperor complained, the Hamburg merchants. . . . But the Admiral did not care. He had decided that if he failed in his more grandiose schemes, he, the husband of the Queen-Dowager of England, would become a pirate !

He made, or rather resumed, another friendship with Sir William Sharington, the keeper of the Bristol Mint. This official, who, with the Admiral, had once been in the service of Sir Francis Bryane, the Vicar of Hell, clipped and sheared the coin, falsified the accounts, made false coin. " The occasion ", he declared, after his arrest, " why I coined festoons was, because I would have the more money in my hands to buy Sylver at Seynt James' Tide, what time there was a great Fair at Bristol " . . . and that silver, again, would be turned into false coins.

Now, in exchange for the Admiral's promise to save him

from punishment should these activities come to light, Sir William agreed to coin £10,000 for the Admiral to use in his seditious adventures.

That protection was never to be extended. The Admiral brought down Sharington with him in his fall. But that was not yet.

To this person the Admiral would boast for hours at a time. He would "look upon a chart of England which he hath, and declare how strong he was ; and how far his Lands and Dominions did stretch . . . and what Shires and Places were for him ; and that this way he was among his friends . . . and when he came to Bristol, he would say, this is my Lord Protector's ; and of other, this is my Lord of Warwick's ; to the which two . . . he had no great affection. And he did vaunt and reckon that he had as great number of Gentlemen that loved him, as any Nobleman in England. And further said, that he had more Gentlemen that loved him, than my Lord Protector." [2]

The Admiral now adopted with the King the attitude of a cat before a caged bird. "Lounging" one morning in St. James's Palace, and seeing the gates open and unguarded, he observed to Fowler that "a man might steal away the King now, for there came more with me than in all the Palace besides".

From lounging, the Admiral turned to roaring threats. At the time of the first Parliament, he said to his cronies Lord Dorset and Lord Clinton, " By God's precious Soul, if I be thus used, I will make this the blackest Parliament that ever was in England". He swore he could live better without the Protector than the Protector could live without him. And that he would " take his fist to the ear of the proudest that should oppose him ".

Rumours of his open insolence, his wild and ferocious threats, having reached the Council, he was summoned to appear before them.

He refused to go. And the Protector did not insist. That kindly weak man seems to have loved his brother, and perhaps from affection, perhaps from inertia, he allowed him to insult with impunity the authority of the Government; and "hoping" (Froude) " that mildness would turn the Admiral, he not only allowed him to retain office at the Admiralty, but gave him further lands ".[3]

But the Admiral's sense of injury increased. " My brother," he declared, " is wondrous hot in helping every man to his right, save me." And his anger was fanned by the Queen, that usually mild-tempered woman, now angered by the fact that the jewels given her by the late King were withheld from her, by other injuries of the sort, and by the open insolence of the Protector's wife.

" Anne, Duchess of Somerset," wrote Hayward,[4] " was a woman for many imperfections intolerable, but for pride monstrous. She was both exceedingly violent and subtle in accomplishing her ends, for which she spurned all respects of conscience and shame. This woman did bear such invincible hatred to the Queen Dowager, first for light causes and women's quarrels, and especially because she, Queen Katherine, had precedency over her." She was, according to Heylin,[5] accustomed to say, " Did not Henry VIII marry Katherine Parr in his doting days, when he had brought himself so low by his lust and cruelty that no lady who stood on her honour would venture on him ? And shall I give place to her, who in her former estate, was but Latimer's widow, and is now fain to cast herself upon a younger brother ? If Master Admiral teach his brother no better manners, I am she that will." And she refused to bear the train of the Queen Dowager as soon as her marriage to the Admiral was made known.

The ladies quarrelled ; the Protector in his weakness, and through his affection for his brother, was pulled, now this way, now that. The Admiral continued his friendship with Sir William Sharington, and his business dealings with Mr. Thompson of Calais. By his secret orders, ships were seized and plundered.

But this was not the only piracy in which the Admiral was interested. At home, in the palace of his wife, was a little girl in her fourteenth year, the daughter of a King. And the Admiral set himself to perform acts of piracy against the emotions, the heart, the future of this child.

In the country palace at Hanworth, to which the households

of the Queen and Princess Elizabeth had removed, Mrs. Ashley, the royal governess, stood listening at an open window of the Princess's bedroom.

We know but little of this lady and her husband — no portrait of them remains to us.

We know, however, that both were much appreciated by Roger Ascham, who, after the death of his friend Grindall, became the tutor of Elizabeth. Sending his " very loving friend Mrs. Ashley " a pen of silver for a token, Ascham expressed " the thanks you have deserved of all true English hearts, for that noble imp " (this meant spray of a tree, and was not used in the modern sense) " by your labour and wisdom now flourisheth in all goodly godliness. . . .

" And although this one thing be sufficient for me to love you, yet the knot which hath knit you and Mr. Ashley together, doth so bind me also to you, that if my ability would match my good will you should find no friend faster. He is a man I loved for his virtue, before I knew him through acquaintance, whose friendship I account among my chief gains gotten at Court. Your favour to Mr. Grindall and gentleness towards me, are matters sufficient enough to deserve more good will than my powers are able to requite."

Mrs. Ashley had a thousand virtues, but discretion was not among them. Her tongue was a babbling brook, and she also, like Lady Bryane, had much of the nature of Juliet's nurse. She could not conceive of a Heaven where there would be neither marrying nor giving in marriage.

At the present moment, however, she was almost frightened into discretion.

As she stood near her charge's open window, darkened against the heat of the sun, shouts of laughter drifted towards her from the gardens, where the Queen and the Admiral were romping with the young Princess.

" Ah." . . . Mrs. Ashley shut her lips together tightly, and gave an angry shudder. . . . For of this conduct she could not approve. Mrs. Ashley could not exactly put her finger on what was wrong, when the behaviour started, soon after the Queen's marriage : but soon it became open, and was talked of. Mrs.

Ashley did not like the conduct of the Admiral towards the Princess.

Now as the little girl rushed upstairs, with scarlet cheeks, and the black cloth dress she wore in mourning for the late King cut into ribbons, Kate Ashley burst out angrily, scolding her, in part, to allay her own anxiety. . . . "What hath your grace done to your gown?" "Oh, how could I help it? — We were wrestling, and the Queen held me while the Admiral cut my gown to pieces."

But Mrs. Ashley continued to scold.

If anything untoward occurred, she would be blamed. And indeed she had, in the past, been singularly indiscreet. Shortly after King Henry's death, she had told Elizabeth, that child of a dangerous inheritance, "If my lord might have had his own will, he would have had you before the Queen". Elizabeth asked her how she knew that, and she replied that she "knew it well enough, both by himself, and by others".[6]

And with those words, something stirred in the darkness of this child's blood and instincts — the summer lightnings of Anne Boleyn's impulses, Henry's incombatable will. Her affections were untouched, but a certain adolescent vanity was half aroused.

"Be careful," Mr. Ashley had said to his wife, when he heard those indiscreet words. "Be careful." . . . He told her he had noticed that Elizabeth blushed, now, when the Admiral was mentioned. . . . But Mrs. Ashley continued to repeat this story to the girl, — not once, but many times.

In the early morning, among the little dark shadows cast by the branches of the rose bush that grew outside the window, a shadow, black, yet glittering as though that shade were encased in armour, would fall across the Princess's bed. . . . Then a boisterous, fine, yet somewhat empty voice was heard. . . . The Admiral had come to say good-morning to his wife's stepdaughter, while she was yet in bed. Sometimes, said Mrs. Ashley in her depositions at the time of the Admiral's trial, he "would make as though he would come at her, and she would go further into her bed, so that he could not come at her".

Though Elizabeth's adolescent vanity had been stirred by

her governess's words, she felt a strong distaste for these coarse familiarities.

One morning, according to the governess, he actually " strove to have kissed her in her bed ". Mrs. Ashley, however, was in the room at the time, and " bade him go away for shame ".

Once, when Mrs. Ashley slept in the Princess's room, the Queen accompanied the Admiral, and they " tytled " (tickled) the Princess as she lay in bed.

At other times, if she were " up and at her books ", he would " bid her good morrow and ax how she did, and strike her upon her Back or the Buttocks familiarly, and so go forth to his lodgings, and sometimes go through to the maides and play with them, and so forth ".[7]

At the Palace at Chelsea, one morning, " the lady Elizabeth (declared her governess), hearing the privy lock undo, knowing that he would come in, ran out of bed to her maidens, and then went behind the curtain of her bed, the maidens being there, and my lord Admirall tarried to have them come out —" (Mrs. Ashley could not say for how long) " and then went his ways ". The ladies complained to her, and she told the Admiral that the household had begun to talk, and that " my lady was evilly spoken of ". She threatened to tell the Protector of his conduct. But the Admiral swore, in his loud voice, his favourite oath : " God's precious soul ! " It was *he* who would complain ! He would tell the Protector he was being slandered. " No, by God, he would not leave it ! " Anyone was welcome to see it ! " What do I ? "[8]

The governess, seeing he had determined to continue in his conduct, told the Queen, who made light of it. Why, the Princess was only a child. . . . " Still," said Mrs. Ashley, " she said she would accompany my lord. And so she did ever after."

. . . Or for a while. She was about to bear a child, and soon the days in which she felt inclined to join in the romps with her stepdaughter were over. The Admiral swore that his expected son " should God give him life to live as long as his father, would avenge his wrongs ".

His wife lay late in her bed these mornings, and the Admiral continued to bid his stepdaughter an early good-morning.

Then, one day, the Palace at Chelsea was full of the sound of whispering. The women looked at each other oddly. It was said that the Queen had sent for Mrs. Ashley and had told her that the Admiral, looking in at the gallery window, " saw my lady Elizabeth with her arms round a man's neck ".

Mrs. Ashley knew that those few bitter words, spoken through half-closed lips, could not be the truth, for, as she said afterwards, " There came no man but Grindall, the lady Elizabeth's schoolmaster." . . . She suspected that " the Queen feigned this, that I might take more heed, and be, as it were, in watch betwixt her " (the Princess) " and the Admiral ".

Long afterwards, she even told the Princess's cofferer, Thomas Parry, in confidence — and withdrew the confidence, as soon as spoken — that " the Admiral had loved the Princess but too well, and had so done a good while " ; and that " the Queen, suspecting too often access of the Admiral to the lady Elizabeth's grace, came suddenly upon them, when they were all alone (he having her in his arms). Whereupon the Queen fell out both with the Lord Admiral and with her Grace also. And thereupon the Queen called me " (Mrs. Ashley) " and told her fancy in this matter, and of this, was much displeasure. . . . And this was not long before they parted asunder their families. . . . I do not know whether . . . she went of herself, or was sent away." [9]

But there seems to have been no open declaration of this at the time, and now we shall never know the true story that lay behind that denunciation, or warning. We do not even know which it was. We only know that, accused by her governess, Elizabeth cried bitterly, and " bade ax all the women ". In answer to every question, she replied with a fresh burst of tears.

If Mrs. Ashley's later story was wrong, whom had this fourteen-year-old girl seen, watching her through the window of the gallery, as she stood clasped in the embrace of a shadow that was no man ? Did she see the bold stare of the Admiral, or was it a ghost that she saw — a young and laughing ghost with black hair and great black slanting eyes — a ghost that laughed at disaster ? Or was it a shrieking ghost in tawdry finery, holding a silk pansy to the place where once her young heart had been

— a ghost that fell silent now as she watched her child-cousin in the arms of a shadow ?

NOTES TO CHAPTER SEVENTEEN

[1] Froude, *Edward VI*.
[2] The Examination of Sir William Sharington.
[3] Act of Attainder of Lord Seymour of Sudeley, Froude, *Edward VI*.
[4] Sir John Hayward, *Life of King Edward VI*.
[5] Heylin, *History of the Reformation*.
[6] The Confession of the Lady Elizabeth, *Domestic Papers Edward VI*, vol. vi.
[7] Confessions of Katherine Ashley, *Domestic Papers Edward VI*, vol. vi.
[8] *Ibid*.
[9] *Ibid*.

Chapter Eighteen

AFTER those few words spoken by the Queen to Mrs. Ashley, there must, one imagines, from Elizabeth's subsequent letter to her stepmother, have been a painful interview between Katherine and her. We do not know what occurred at that interview, — reproaches or warnings. But Elizabeth seems to have felt gratitude. And yet — to some of us it is more easy to forgive one who has done us a terrible injury, than to forgive the loving unsuspecting being who has received such a blow from our hands. Therefore, the feeling Elizabeth had for her stepmother *may* have changed. One does not know, nor does one know what was the agony of betrayed love in the heart of Katherine. Perhaps, again, Elizabeth may have hated the Admiral's behaviour, — and Katherine may have known this.

In any case, after that interview, one would not have been aware that anything had happened,—although the whole of life had changed.

For nothing must be known of this in the outer world, since, if the Protector and the Council came to hear of it, the Admiral's downfall would be a certainty. And what would be said of Elizabeth — the child of Anne Boleyn ?

The Queen was about to bear a child, and it was natural, therefore, that at Whitsuntide (a few weeks after those interviews) Elizabeth and her train should remove from the Queen's household to Cheshunt.

From there, the girl wrote this letter to her stepmother :

" Although I could not be plentiful in giving thanks for the manifold kindnesses received at your Highness's hand, at my departure, yet I am something to be borne withall, for truly I was replete with sorrow to depart from your Highness, especially seeing you undoubtful of health, and albeit I answered little, I weighed it deeply when you said — you would warn me of all evilnesses that you should hear of me, for if your Grace had not a good opinion of me — you would not have offered friendship to me that way at all — meaning the contrary. But what may I more say than thank God for providing such friends for me, desiring God to enrich me with their loving life, and your grace to be in heart no less thankful to receive it than I am now made glad in writing to show it. And although I have plenty of matter here, I will stay, for I know you are not quick to read.

from Cheston, this present Saturday

your Highness's humble daughter

Elizabeth."

What feeling underlies this letter ? . . . Gratitude that the Queen had understood that what had happened was not her fault ? — or shame that for one moment she had been betrayed into an unthinking disloyalty to the stepmother who had loved her like a daughter ? I think the former. And surely this is proved by the fact that after Katherine's death it was found she had left Elizabeth, in her will, half her jewels and " a rich chain of gold ".

Nothing had happened. Life went outwardly on as if that terrible day had never been !

Other of Elizabeth's letters to the Queen had a tender, even a playful note. Nor was the Admiral excluded from the correspondence ; Elizabeth wrote him amiable notes, of a formal friendliness.

But three months after Elizabeth's departure from her stepmother's household, the Queen lay dying, at Sudeley Castle, after the birth of that much-hoped-for child — that was a girl — not " a son to avenge his father's wrongs ".

" Two days before the death of the Queen," said Lady Tyrwhit, her stepdaughter by her first husband Lord Brough, and her friend and attendant — " at my coming to her in the morning, she asked me ' Where I had been so long ', and said unto me ' that she did fear such things in herself that she was sure she could not live '. I answered, as I thought, that I saw no likelihood of death in her. She then, having my lord Admiral by the hand, and divers others standing by, spake these words, partly, as I took, idly " (i.e. in delirium) : " ' My Lady Tyrwhit, I am not well handled, for those that are about me care not for me, but stand laughing at my grief, and the more good I will to them, the less good they will to me'. Whereunto, my lord Admiral answered, ' Why, sweetheart ! I would you no hurt ! ' And she said to him again, aloud, ' No my lord, I think so '. And immediately she said in his ear, ' But, my lord, you have given me many shrewd taunts ! ' These words I perceived she spake with good memory, and very sharply and earnestly ; for her mind was sore disquieted. My lord Admiral, perceiving that I heard it, called me aside, and asked me what she said, and I declared plainly to him. Then he consulted with me that he would lie down on the bed by her, to look if he could pacify her unquietness with gentle communication, — whereunto I agreed ; And by the time that he had spoken three or four words to her, she answered sharply, saying, ' My lord, I would have given a thousand marks to have had my full talk with Hewyke * the first day I was delivered, but I durst not for displeasing you ! ' And I, hearing that, perceived her trouble to be so great, that my heart would serve me to hear no more. Such like communication she had with him the space of an hour, which they did hear that sat by her bedside."

From this arose the charge, whispered at first, then declared openly, that the Admiral had poisoned his wife. It is quite unfounded, nor is there any reason to believe that the illness consequent on the child's birth was aggravated by his unkindness. On the contrary, he seems to have shown her great tenderness, and even patience for her sick fancies. The dying woman imagined, perhaps, as Miss Strickland thinks may have been the case, that in a dark corner of her lying-in room people were muttering to each other of her husband's passion for Elizabeth, — saying, perhaps, that he wished his wife were dead, that he might marry the girl he loved. . . . Yes, it was surely that which was being whispered in the corners. . . . They were laughing at her, because, after all, happiness had not come to her.

" Her malady ", said Miss Strickland,[1] " was evidently fever, brought on by distress of mind ; a sense of intolerable wrong

* Hewyke was her physician.

was constantly expressed by her, yet she never explained the cause of her displeasure."

So she lay dying, with her hair that had been golden as the kingcups of spring, dulled by her pain and the dews of death. . . . Three hundred years or so after this time, her biographer, Agnes Strickland, saw " a lock of hair which had been broken from the head of Queen Katherine Parr, after it had lain in the dust and darkness of the grave for nearly two centuries and a half. . . . It was of the most exquisite quality and colour, exactly resembling threads of burnished gold in its hue. . . . It was discovered that a wreath of ivy had twined itself round the temples of the royal corpse, a berry having fallen there and taken root at the time of her previous exhumation, and there had silently, from day to day, woven itself into this green coronal. . . ."

Katherine Parr died on the 5th of September 1548, two days before her stepdaughter's fifteenth birthday.

The news of the Queen's death was brought to Elizabeth by one Edward, a servant of the Admiral's, who described to the household, at great length, the Admiral's sorrow. . . . "His lord", he said, "was a heavy man." . . . But when Mrs. Ashley, full of excitement, urged her charge to write a letter of condolence to the widower — "I will not do it," she replied, "for he needs it not."

She was thinking, perhaps, of those early morning visits. "Then if your Grace will not," said Mrs. Ashley, "then will I." And she did, showing the letter to Elizabeth, who, with no comment, allowed it to be sent.

Lady Tyrwhit now re-enters the story. . . . We saw her first, bending over the deathbed of the Queen; but now, although the dead woman was hardly laid in her grave, she said to Mrs. Ashley, "that it was the opinion of many that the lord Admiral kept the late Queen's maidens together to wait on the lady Elizabeth, whom he intended shortly to marry".

Perhaps this was a trap, laid by that virtuous and unworldly lady. In any case Mrs. Ashley had been warned by her husband: "Take heed, for it" (the Princess's marriage) "were but undoing, if it were done without the Council's leave".

The usually garrulous Mrs. Ashley listened, therefore, to Lady Tyrwhit's speech in silence.

But Lady Tyrwhit was not the only person interested. A fussy Polonius-like being, Sir Nicholas Throckmorton (a cousin by marriage of the late Queen), had a confidential conversation with one of the Admiral's servants, Wightman ; and he, flattered by the attention paid him, agreed with Sir Nicholas that any attempt on the part of the Admiral to marry the Princess would be fatal.

The rumours grew, and with them Mrs. Ashley's excitement, her sense of importance. One Sir Henry Parker sent his servant to ask the truth of the report. Mrs. Ashley returned the answer " that he should in no wise credit it, for it was ne thought, ne meant ". But this again was merely an unnatural discretion. She bustled about, doing her utmost to awaken Elizabeth's interest in the widower.

The governess, and the cofferer, Thomas Parry, talked of nothing but the Admiral — of his feeling for Elizabeth, of the romantic situation. For the Admiral had completely won over these persons : Mrs. Ashley's indignation over the morning visits was now forgotten. She had always (she told herself) wished to see Elizabeth the bride of the Admiral. . . . Such a fine man, so handsome, and with such a presence — and so deeply in love ! And now it would come to pass. Why, it was like a fairy-tale !

Mrs. Ashley had been the governess of Elizabeth since her earliest childhood ; the girl believed in her judgment, trusted her, loved her. She was Elizabeth's Oracle, — and next to her, in Elizabeth's estimation, was the cofferer.

It was natural that to a young girl of Elizabeth's age, these stories of romance, of faithful love rewarded, of the happy ending to a fairy tale, would have their effect. Elizabeth began to fancy herself in love with the Admiral — or, perhaps, to wish that she was in love with him.

The fairy-tale theme would have been a little dimmed if she could have seen the behaviour of the hero when he was not on the stage.

" When I went unto my lord Admiral the third and fourth time," said Parry, in his examination, " after he had asked me how her Grace did, and such things, he questioned me of many things, and of the state of her Grace's house, and how many servants she kept ; and I told him 120, or 140, or thereabouts. Then he asked me what houses she had, and what lands ? . . . He asked me if they were good lands or no, and whether she had the bonds for them for life, or what ? " . . .

The Admiral fell to comparing his housekeeping with that of the Princess, and said he could do it with less expense. . . . In his lazy way, he said that when her Grace came to Ashridge it was not far out of his way, and he might come to see her on his way up and down, and he would he glad to see her there. Parry told him that he " could not go to see her Grace till he knew what her pleasure was ". " Why ? " said the Admiral. " It is no matter now, for there hath been a talk of late that I shall marry the Lady Jane," adding, " I tell you this merrily — I tell you this merrily ! "

The Admiral hoped, no doubt, that this would be repeated to Elizabeth, and might arouse jealousy in her. For Lady Jane Grey, after an effort on the part of her mother to have her removed from the Admiral's house, on the death of the Queen, had remained there under the care of the Admiral's mother, who was now in charge of the household.

Thomas Parry returned to Hatfield ; but whether he repeated the saying of the Admiral or not, is unknown. What is certain is that the time and energy spent by the Admiral in winning the favour of that indiscreet pair, the governess and the cofferer, were amply repaid. . . . The governess was no longer afraid that the Queen might suspect a half-developed, or a possible, situation. For the Queen was dead, and could no longer approve or disapprove. The Duchess of Somerset, however, was alive, — a Megaera, a termagant, with the irrationality and the energy of a storm of wind. . . . The Duchess of Somerset, who hated her brother-in-law, and hated, still worse, his dead wife, who, as Queen-Dowager, had taken precedence of her.

The Duchess sent for Mrs. Ashley, and scolded her because " she had permitted my lady Elizabeth's grace to go one night on the Thames in a barge, and for other light parts ", saying

N

" that she was not worthy to have the governance of a King's daughter ! "

For the moment, Mrs. Ashley was not only abashed, but frightened. Then she continued on the way she had chosen.

But everyone was not won as easily as the indiscreet household of the Princess. . . .

One day, as the Admiral rode with Lord Russell, the Lord Privy Seal, from the Protector's house to Parliament House, the Admiral said, " Father Russell, you are very suspicious or me ; I pray you tell me, who showed you of the marriage that I should attempt, whereof ye brake with me the other day ? " Russell, after some conversation, said, " My lord, I shall earnestly advise you to make no suit for marriage that way ! " Said the Admiral, " It is convenient for them " (the Princesses) " to marry, and better it were they were married within the realm than in any foreign place and without " (outside) " the realm. And why might not I, or another, made by the King their father, marry one of them ? "

Lord Russell answered, " My Lord, if either you or any other within the realm, shall match himself in marriage, either with my lady Mary, or with my lady Elizabeth, undoubtedly, whatsoever he be, he shall procure unto himself the occasion oₓ his utter undoing ; and you especially, being of so near alliance to the King's Majesty ".

Upon the Admiral enquiring what he meant, Lord Russell reminded him that the King's father " was a prince of much wisdom and knowledge, yet was very suspicious and given to suspect. The King's grandfather also, King Henry VII, was a very noble and wise prince, but he also was very suspicious." . . . Was it not likely, therefore, that the young King might inherit this suspicious nature ? And if the Admiral, being related to his Highness, should also marry one of the heirs of the crown by succession, might the King not hold him suspect, and "as often as he shall see you, think that you gape and wish for his death " ?

Lord Russell added, " And I pray you, my lord, what shall you have with any of them ? " (as marriage portion). The Admiral replied that " who married one of them should have three thousand a year ".

" By God," roared Lord Russell, " but they may not ! "

" By God," answered the Admiral, roaring yet louder, " none of you all dare say nay to it ! "

Lord Russell, reporting the speech, declared, " I answered, ' By God ! for my part *I* will say nay to it ; for it is clean against the King's will '."

And they parted.

The Admiral was unabashed. He talked openly to the Earl of Rutland about putting an end to the Protectorate. And believing that Wriothesley bore a grudge against the Protector for the loss of the Chancellorship, the Admiral swore, should he come into power, to restore the office to him. But to his surprise, Wriothesley answered : " For God's sake, my lord, heed what you do ; I hear abroad that you make a party ". " Marry, I would have things better ordered," said the Admiral. " My lord," said Wriothesley, " beware how you attempt any violence. It were better that you had never been born, yea, that you had been burned alive quick, than that you should attempt it."

When Elizabeth wished to go to London to spend Christmas at Court, she was at a loss where to reside, for Durham House, given by King Henry to her mother before the marriage, had been taken by the Council and converted into a mint. The gallant Admiral, on hearing this, offered to give up his own house for her use, adding " that he would come and see her Grace ". " Which declaration ", said Parry, " she seemed to take very gladly, and to accept it joyfully."

The cofferer had noticed that her face showed signs of pleasure when the Admiral was mentioned, and he asked her " whether, if the Council would like it, she would marry with him ".

She replied that she would not tell him her mind, and enquired further what he meant by asking her that question, and who told him to do so. He answered, " Nobody ".

This was about a fortnight before Christmas.

At the time of the Admiral's arrest, Parry, also under arrest, remembered that when he told Elizabeth that the Admiral would like to exchange lands with her, she asked him " what he meant thereby ". He replied, "I cannot tell, unless he go about to have you also, for he wished your lands and would have them that way ".

Elizabeth did not answer.

Parry then informed her that the Admiral wished her to go to the Duchess of Somerset, and beg her to " make suit to the Protector for the exchange of the lands, and to a grant to herself of a house in the place of Durham House ". . . . . The royal girl replied, " I daresay he did not say so, nor would ".

" Yes, by my faith," said Parry.

" Well," said she, with anger in her voice, " I will not do so, and so tell him. In faith, I will not come there, nor begin to flatter now."

The strange greatness of phrase which was to be a mark of this Fate-stricken creature, had begun, even in early youth, to show the buds that would soon break into splendour.

Then the conversation shifted slightly, and the Princess asked Parry if he had told Mrs. Ashley of the Admiral's kindness, and his offer. " I told her ' no '," said Parry in his examination.

" Well," said the Princess, " go tell it her, for I will know nothing but she shall know it. In faith I cannot be quiet until ye have told her of it."

The governess, when this was repeated, said " she knew it well enough ". Parry answered " that it seemed to him that there was goodwill between the lord Admiral and her grace, and that he gathered this both by him and her grace ". " Oh yes," exclaimed Mrs. Ashley, " it is true ; but " (remembering her scolding from the Duchess of Somerset) " I had such a charge that I dare nothing say in it ; but I would wish her his wife of all men living. I wis he might bring the matter to pass at the Council's hands well enough."

And she fell to praising the Admiral. . . . Parry (according to his own account) said idly, that for all that, " he heard very ill reports of the Admiral, that he was very covetous, and an oppressor, and had an evil jealousy — and that he had treated the late Queen cruelly, dishonestly, and jealously ".

" Tush, tush," quoth she, " it is no matter. I know him better than you, or those who so report him. I know he will make but too much of her, and that she knows well enough." . . .

And she began to gossip about the Admiral's jealousy over the late Queen.

Having gone so far, Mrs. Ashley went a little further.

This conversation took place on Twelfth Night. . . . Both Mrs. Ashley and the cofferer felt in a confidential mood. After a long, comfortable gossip, Mrs. Ashley told the cofferer her version of the disturbance at Chelsea.

Parry drank it in eagerly. "Why," he said, "hath there been such familiarity between them?" Mrs. Ashley only sighed and said, "I will tell you more another time." "But," she added, "if the King's majesty that dead is, had lived a little longer, she would have been his wife."

With those words, she seems to have had some inkling of the baseness of her disclosure about the young girl in her charge. . . . But what she had done could never be undone. She could only pray the cofferer never to repeat, in any way, any part of what she had told him. He swore he would not. But again she begged him not to — not for anything in the world must he reveal it. . . . For her grace would be dishonoured for ever.

Parry swore that he would rather be pulled asunder by wild horses than divulge what she had told him.

But it was from him — at the time of the Admiral's arrest — that the Council knew these matters. And so the story has come down to us.

Either the day after Twelfth Night, or on that following, Parry paid a visit to the Admiral.

He was shown into the Admiral's room. The Admiral said, "How doth her grace?" And Parry said, "Well". Then the Admiral asked when she would be coming to London. Parry replied that "My Lord Protector's grace was not determined upon the day". "No," quoth he : "that shall be when I am gone to Boulogne." "Sir," Parry said, "Mistress Ashley commends her unto you, and hath bidden me tell you she is your friend as she was." "Oh," he exclaimed, "I know she is my friend." "Sir," continued Parry, "she would her Grace were your wife of any man living." "Oh," he answered, "it will not be ; My brother will not agree to it." And he muttered something under his breath — " I am kept back," or " I am kept under." But Parry could not hear for certain, because the Admiral stammered the words out. " But I pray you let me know when she comes up ; and come another time," added the Admiral.

It struck Parry that the Admiral was " in some heat, or very busy, or had some mistrust of me ".

Had Thomas Parry but known it, he was seeing that gallant, swashbuckling, loud-voiced figure, that glittering shadow cast across the young life of Elizabeth, for the last time.

NOTE TO CHAPTER EIGHTEEN

[1] Strickland, *Catherine Parr.* (Lives of the Queens of England.)

Chapter Nineteen

ON the night of the 17th of January the Admiral sat in his house, waiting for the men who would soon visit him. He knew that they were coming, for he had been warned of this by one of his retainers.

The hours passed ; and still he waited. Would the knock at the door never come ? Hour after hour. . . .

Some time before this, he had sworn to Lord Warwick, " By God's precious soul, whosoever lays hands on me, I shall thrust my dagger in him ". But when, at last, the guard came to arrest him, he did not draw his sword. Violently protesting his innocence, swearing with many oaths that " he had attempted nothing against the King — on the contrary, he had the King's confidence and approval ", he was hustled from the room, and into a barge ; and so on to the Tower.

The King's Council was summoned to discuss whether the Lord High Admiral, Lord Seymour of Sudeley, should be arraigned on a charge of high treason.

Then the little boy who had been kept short of pocket-money — the King's Majesty —, said these words : " We do perceive that there be great things which be objected and laid to my Lord Admiral mine uncle, and they tend to treason ; we perceive that you require but justice to be done ; we think it reasonable, and we will that you proceed according to your request ".

" With these words coming so suddenly from his grace's mouth of his own motion, as the lords might well perceive, the said lords and the rest of the Council were marvellously rejoiced, and gave his highness most hearty praise and thanks." [1]

His highness also told in full the story of his uncle's transactions with him — the gifts of pocket-money, the complaints about the Protector, the attempts to make him sign papers, the instigations to defiance.

The Admiral was brought before both Houses of Parliament

(the Bill against him having been drawn) . . . and the accusations were read to him.

The first charge was made : that he had attempted to gain possession of the King's person. This he admitted : he had intended to bring a motion before the House of Lords, — for there were precedents of which he was aware — " but Sir William Paget had made him ashamed of his doings, and he had left his labour ". . . . As to giving the boy money, yes, he admitted that too — (he could hardly do otherwise, after the King's disclosures) — and he had tried to persuade Edward to write a letter to the Parliament " expressing a wish that the government should be changed ".[2] After this, he adopted a policy of muteness. About the other and more serious charges, he would say nothing. " I have confessed enough," was all that could be drawn from him.

Seeing the Admiral committed for treason, his confederates threw up the game. Sir William Sharington confessed, not only the Admiral's dealings with him, but his own private forgeries and depletions, — throwing himself upon the Protector's mercy.

The weak Dorset, the Admiral's intimate crony, terrified of the position in which he found himself, told all : the Admiral's arrangement by which he bought the custody of Lady Jane Grey, in order that she might live in his house — his wish to marry her to the King.

One person alone seems to have tried to save the Admiral — a gentleman of his service named Harington. During the reign of Elizabeth, the Queen became godmother to the son of this faithful and gallant man, who married one of her maids of honour. This godchild was the " boy Jack " to whom she showed innumerable kindnesses — perhaps in gratitude to the man who had tried to save one who died because of her. In memory, too, of the subsequent time when Harington became her fellow prisoner, for her sake.

Harington swore that he had heard the Admiral say, if he were offered the Protectorate or the governorship of the King, he wished the earth would open and swallow him if he would take it. As for the Council, he had said nothing against them.

Perhaps he might have said " This man or that was my friend ",
— but where founding a Party was concerned, he had never
mentioned it. With regard to the plan to marry Lady Jane
Grey to the King, — the Admiral had said, merely, it would
do her no harm to live in the house of the King's uncle, and if
the King should like anyone in his house, he would be very glad.
But he understood the other was dangerous . . . and therefore
entered not into it. — The Admiral had never said the King
disliked his Government. — The Admiral had said, one day,
" Indeed I have some occasion to think unkindness in him "
(the Protector) " if I would so take it ; for he keepeth away the
Queen's jewels, the which I might attempt to recover by the
Law if I would . . . but I would rather they were on fire than
I would attempt this ".

Harington continued : " Coming in the boat with my Lord
Admiral on his way to the Council, my Lord had said : " I am
sure I can have no hurt, if they do me right ; they cannot kill
me except they do me wrong ; and if they do, I shall die but
once, and if they take my life from me, I have a Master who
will avenge ".

He was asked if he knew that " my lord Admiral went about
any marriage for himself ".

He answered, " No ! "

In the Princess's household at Hatfield there was blank terror
and amazement.

" Upon sudden news that my lord Great Master and Master
Denny were arrived at the gate, the Cofferer turned horribly
pale, went hastily to his chamber, and said to my lady his wife,
' I would I had never been born, for I am undone ' — and
wrung his hands, and cast away his chain from his neck and
his rings from his fingers." [3]

The cofferer and Mrs. Ashley were arrested and taken away.
. . . And the fifteen-year-old daughter of Anne Boleyn, the
stepdaughter of Katherine Howard, was left with these ghosts
for company.

She was left friendless, but not alone.

A new governess, Lady Tyrwhit, arrived, and with her, that
governess's husband, Sir Robert Tyrwhit.

This melancholy, grimly pious, acidulated pair had been sent as spies, to discover Elizabeth's actions, present and past, to worm their way into her very thoughts, and the feelings of her heart.

Lady Tyrwhit met with a freezing reception.

The Princess told her that Mrs. Ashley was her mistress, and that she had not so demeaned herself that the Council should now need to put any more mistresses over her : to which Lady Tyrwhit replied that as she allowed Mrs. Ashley to be her mistress, " she need not be ashamed to have any honest woman in her place ". (She had previously told the Princess that the Council had sent for her and rebuked her that she had not taken upon herself the office to see Elizabeth well governed in lieu of Mrs. Ashley, — for Lady Tyrwhit had been one of the late Queen's ladies-in-waiting, and probably knew of the governess's indiscretions while at Chelsea.)

The girl took the matter so heavily that, according to the spies, " she wept all that night, and lowered all the next day ". . . .

The male spy perceived that she was very loth to have a governor, " and to avoid the same, said the world would note her to be a great offender, having so hastily a governess appointed her ". He added that this was because she " fully hopes to recover her old mistress again. The love she yet beareth her is to be wondered at. . . ."

The wife was merely doleful ; but the husband attempted to terrify this helpless girl, with the fate of her mother and of Katherine Howard ever in her mind, into a confession that would inculpate, not only herself, but the Admiral, Kate Ashley whom she loved, and Parry whom, however mistakenly, she trusted.

One false step, on the part of this fifteen-year-old girl . . . then the Tower,—the headsman's block for herself, and for others.

But Sir Robert and his wife did not feel that they were making much headway. The knight, therefore, asked the Protector if Lady Browne (Fair Geraldine, of Surrey's poems) might go to the Princess's household as an extra spy, since he thought that Elizabeth might trust and confide in her, and be led by her to make confession.

The next move on the part of this high-minded man was (according to his own proud account), to " devise a letter to Mistress Blanche " (possibly Blanche Parry, the cofferer's daughter) from a friend of hers, to say that both Mrs. Ashley and the cofferer had been taken to the Tower.

This forged letter was shown to Elizabeth, — and she, said Sir Robert, " did weep very tenderly a long time ".

In her agony of mind, she asked Lady Browne (who, it would seem, showed her the letter) if they had confessed any-thing — words which were repeated immediately by this woman. Then the Princess sent for Sir Robert, and told him there were certain things she had forgotten to disclose, but which should be laid before the Protector. . . . One was, that at the end of a letter written on her behalf by the cofferer to the Admiral, asking some benefit for her chaplain Alleyn, she had suggested that the Admiral should be " suitor " to the Protector for Durham Place ; another was that there had been some discussion in a letter written by Mrs. Ashley, about a visit from the Admiral . . . insignificant points. . . .

Sir Robert Tyrwhit then required this daughter of Anne Boleyn to " consider her Honour, and the Peril that might ensue, *for she was but a subject* ". . . .

That sentence must have followed Elizabeth through the long nights to come.

Tyrwhit, describing to the Protector the subsequent con-versation, wrote : " And I have declared what a woman Mrs. Ashley was ". . . . He added that if the Princess would confess, openly, everything that had happened, " all the evil and shame should be ascribed to them " (*i.e.* Mrs. Ashley and Parry), " and her youth considered both with the King's Majesty, your Grace, and the whole Council. But in no ways she will not [*sic*] confess any practise by Mrs. Ashley or the Cofferer, concerning the Lord Admiral, — and yet I do see in her face that she is guilty, and do perceive as yet she will abide more storms, ere she eschew Mrs. Ashley." [4]

By the evening of the 23rd, in spite of incessant questioning, all he had been able to extract from this young girl was the story that the Admiral had offered to lend her his house that she might come to London to see the King, — and the cofferer's subsequent question whether, should the Council consent, she would accept the Admiral as her husband. Sir Robert had hoped that more could be wrung from her, but as he told the Protector, "I do assure your Grace that she hath a very good wit, and nothing is gotten of her, but by great policy." . . .

On the 28th, he was obliged to tell the Protector that by no means could he induce the Princess to confess more than she had done . . . "she doth plainly deny that she knoweth any more". He added, "I do believe that there hath been some secret promise between my Lady, Mistress Ashley, and the Cofferer, never to confess till death ; and if it be so, it will never be gotten of her, but either by the King's Majesty, or else by your Grace."

By this time, Sir Robert and " my Lady's Controller, Master Beverley ", had gone over the account of the cofferer's clerks . . . "which were found very uncertain, and his Books so indiscreetly made, that it doth well appear that he had little understanding to execute his office ". Sir Robert told the Princess she must retrench on the expenses of her household. The girl, in reply, asked that no new cofferer should be appointed at present. The work could be done by a clerk, and this, she said, would save her a hundred a year.

An excuse, as Sir Robert well knew, so that Parry's place should not be filled.

On the same day as that on which the Protector was told of these household matters, the Princess, then aged fifteen and a quarter, wrote him a letter. After asseverating her innocence, and the innocence of her governess and cofferer, she ends the letter thus : "Master Tyrwhit and others have told me that there goeth rumours abroad, which be both equally against my Honour and Honesty (which above all other things I esteem), which be these : That I am in the Tower ; and with child by my Lord Admiral. My Lord, these are shameful Slanders, for the which, besides the great desire I have to see the King's Majesty, I heartily desire your Lordship that I may come to Court, after your first determination, that I may show myself as I am."

In that letter, we recognise the true Elizabethan greatness.

So began that long and calumniated life — that life of faithful and betrayed love, of self-abnegation. It began with a slander, and the stain of that slander yet remains upon her.

Her childhood had been one filled with fear — but now the fear had come more close. It had been advancing, step by step, in those months when the Admiral was making his only partly understood advances. Sometimes Fear wore the Admiral's face for mask.

Still, by the 7th of February, Elizabeth had not been brought to say one thing of any importance which could reflect on Mrs. Ashley or Parry.

But Mrs. Ashley and Parry were very different beings from the Tudor Princess. They, and in particular Parry, told everything which could reflect discredit upon the young girl who had been in their charge. Parry was the first traitor : Mrs. Ashley only spoke when she thought all was lost, through the cofferer's disclosures.

But in any case, she repeated the story of the Admiral's early morning visits, with full details.

The confessions of this pair were made to the Council, and the rumours grew. . . . It was said, by the gossips, not only that Elizabeth had been seduced by the Admiral, and was about to bear a child, but that she had already borne him one. In the *Life of Jane Dormer*, then a maid of honour to Princess Mary, and afterwards Duchess of Feria, it is written, " There was a report of a child born and miserably destroyed, but that it could not be discovered whose it was. A midwife testified that she was brought from her house, blindfold, to a house where she did her office, and returned in like manner. She saw nothing in the house but candle-light, and only said it was the child of a very fair young lady."

The very fair young lady must, necessarily, have been Elizabeth. Who else ?

Sir Robert, in his attempt to turn Elizabeth against her governess and cofferer, and in the hope of obtaining further admissions, showed the girl their confessions made to the Council . . . those which detailed the behaviour of the Admiral while she was living under his roof.

"At the reading of Mistress Ashley's letters," the spy told his master, "she was much abashed, and half breathless, ere she could read it to an end ; and perused all their names " (perhaps at first she could not credit such base cowardice, and thought it must be some new trick, some forgery) ". . . and knew both Mrs. Ashley's hand and the Cofferer's within half a sight, so that fully she thinketh they have both confessed all they know. When I declared to her, that Mrs. Ashley would utter nothing, until Parry and she were brought face to face, when he stood fast to, of all he had written ; she seeing that, called him false wretch, and said that he had promised he would never confess it to death. Her answer was to this, ' that it was a great matter for him to promise such a Promise, and to break it '."

The above report, owing to the extremely strange construction of Sir Robert's sentences, has caused confusion. Actually, it was ·Mrs. Ashley who called the cofferer " false wretch ". But the mistaken idea has arisen that Elizabeth was the speaker, and that therefore the cofferer was in *her* confidence, and knew from *her* lips some guilty secret. . . .

She knew they had done her a deadly injury. And yet this noble girl not only forgave them — understanding, perhaps, their terror, — but wrote to the Protector begging him to have mercy upon Mrs. Ashley.

" My Lord," the letter ran, " I have a request to make unto your grace which fear has made me omit till this time for two causes — the one because I saw that my request for the rumours which were spread of me took so little place, which thing when I considered I thought I should little profit in any other suit, howbeit, now I understand that there is a Proclamation for them (for the which I give your Grace and the rest of the Council most hearty thanks) I am the bolder to speak for another thing ; and the other was because peradventure your Lordship and the Council will think that I favour her evil doing whom I shall speak for, which is for Katheryn Ashley, that it will please your Grace and the Council to do good unto her. Which thing I do not to favour her in any evil (for that I would be sorry to do) but for these considerations which follow. . . . First, because she hath been with me a long time, and many years, and hath taken great labour, and pain in bringing me up in learning and honesty — and therefore I ought of my duty to speak for her, for Saint Gregory sayeth that we are more bound to them that bring us up well, than to our parents, for our parents do that which is natural for them, that is, bringeth us into this world, but our bringers up are a cause to make us live well in it. The second is because I think that whatsoever she hath done in my Lord Admiral's matter as concerning the marriage for me, she hath done it because knowing him to be one of the Council, she thought he would not go about any such thing without he had the Council's consent thereto ; for I have heard her many times say that she would never have me marry in any place without your Grace's and the Council's consent. The third is because that it shall and doth make men think that I am not clear of the deed myself, but that it is pardoned on me because of my youth, because that she I loved so well is in such a place.

"Thus hope, prevailing more in me than fear, hath won the battle ; and I have at this time gone forth with it, which I pray God be taken no other ways than it is meant. Written in haste. From Hatfield the 7th day of March. Also if I may be so bold not offending I beseech your Grace and the rest of the Council to be good to Master Ashley her husband, which because he is my kinsman I would be glad he should be well.

Your assured friend to my little power

Elizabeth."

In answer to the Protector's tardy offer to punish those spreading evil reports about her, if she would say who had done so, she refused it, saying it would get " the evil will of the people, which I would be loathe to have. But if it might seem good unto your Lordship and the rest of the Council, to send forth a proclamation to the counties that they refrain their tongues, declaring that the tales be but lies, it should make both the people think that you and the Council have great regard that no such rumours should be spread of one of the King's Majesty's sisters, as I am, though unworthy ! "

After this rebuke, she added, " Concerning that you say that I give folks occasion to think, in refusing the good to uphold the evil, I am not of so simple understanding ".

Sir Robert Tyrwhit told the Protector that the Princess had begun to droop, knowing that the Admiral's household had been disbanded — and knowing what that meant. — If he was mentioned, she defended him, nor would hear one word in his disfavour.

She knew now that the Admiral must die. There was no hope, there was no help.

Each morning, after a sleepless night, she rose, grey and drooping with fatigue, and throughout the day, Lady Tyrwhit's exhortations and prayers, that took the form of lamentations, circled round and round in Elizabeth's head — empty now even of anguish, — like a bird that had lost its way and was imprisoned in an empty room. " Woe is me," ran one prayer, " careful carcase and born in sin ; deprived of original justice, compared to a beast, is Adam fallen as a rotten apple from a living tree. What have I gotten by my fall ? Darkness, care, misery, affliction, sickness, pain, anguish, and finally dreadful death. And alas ! What shall I be hereafter ? A stinking carrion, worms' meat, food for fire, dust and clay, dung and forsaken, rotten and consumed, blind, poor and naked." . . . So ran one of these communications with God (" Monuments of Matrons ").

" Forsaken . . . Forsaken . . . Forsaken . . ."

The words circled round in Elizabeth's mind, blundering into the light, then back into the darkness again.

On the 17th of March, Seymour was told by the Bishop of Ely that his death was approaching.

His last hours were spent in writing to Elizabeth and Mary, urging them to conspire against his brother. For fear lest the letters should be found by the authorities and withheld from the Princesses, he hid them in the sole of a shoe ; and when about to place his head upon the block, his last words were to his servant, telling him to remember the letters. . . . But his words, though muttered, were overheard, the servant examined, and the letters taken from him. The pen with which they were written was " the aglet of a point that he plucked from his hose ".

He died with great bravery, after more than one stroke of the axe.

" As touching the kind of his death," said Latimer, in the sermon preached before the little King, " I refer that to God. In the twinkling of an eye He may save a man, and turn his heart. What he did I cannot tell. And when a man hath two strokes with an axe, who can tell but between two strokes he doth repent ? It is hard to judge. But this I will say, if they ask me what I think of his death, that he died very dangerously, irksomely, and horribly. He was a wicked man, and the realm is well rid of him." . . .

Perhaps on the night following that death, Elizabeth may have slept well for the first time since this terror had begun. So does one sleep when all hope is over.

Seeing her, lying there, you would never have guessed how she would look, fifty-five-odd years after that time, when she was a very old woman, waiting for death. . . . For now she is peaceful, and not affrighted because she had seen her own body (as she was to do), " exceeding lean and fearful, in a light of fire ", lying in her bed. . . . The old sandalwood body, dying, and smelling of death. . . . But now her cheek is rounded, and she will not wake saying, as she said, two years before her end, when there were rumours that her death had already occurred, " Mortua sed non sepulta. Mortua sed non sepulta ". . . . (" Dead but not buried. Dead but not buried.")

Looking at her now, sleeping so quietly, you can hear no sound from that peaceful heart, of " the drums and tramplings of a hundred conquests " — nor could you foretell that terrible end.

" I found ", wrote a contemporary, " her disease to be nothing but a settled melancholy, inasmuch as she could not be . . . persuaded, neither by Councils, Divines, Physicians, nor the Women about her, once to sup, or touch any Physic. . . . She held an obstinate silence, for the most part, because she had a persuasion that if she once lay down she should never rise ; could not be got to go to bed for a whole week, till three days before her death." — Lady Southwell, her devoted lady-in-waiting, speaks of "the three days she sat upon a stool" ; adding that "one day, being pulled up by force, she obstinately stood on her feet for fifteen hours ".[5]

She who had fought the power of Spain, the power of the Pope, she who had said to the Swedish Ambassador (then threatening her of the dangers she would incur if she did not marry his master), "I have the heart of a man, not a woman, and I am not afraid of anything" — was now facing her last enemy, Death. She who had loved two things — England and Leicester — must give her heart to Death.

But now she is a young girl, sleeping soundly after her first sorrow.

The great, the terrible tomorrow had not yet invaded her heart.

NOTES TO CHAPTER NINETEEN

[1] *Literary Remains of Edward VI.*
[2] Froude, *Edward VI.*
[3] Sir Robert Tyrwhit to the Lord Protector, Haynes, vol. iii.
[4] Tyrwhit to the Lord Protector, January 22.
[5] Quoted by Strickland, *Elizabeth.*